The Phonogram in Cultural Communication

Report on a Research Project
Undertaken by Mediacult

Edited by K. Blaukopf

Springer-Verlag
Wien New York

Kurt Blaukopf
Director, MEDIACULT, International Institute for Audio-Visual
Communication and Cultural Development, Wien, Austria

This study was carried out and published with the financial assistance of
the International Fund for the Promotion of Culture of UNESCO.

With 4 Figures

© 1982 by Springer-Verlag Wien

Printed in Austria

Library of Congress Cataloging in Publication Data. Main entry under title: The
Phonogram in cultural communication. 1. Sound recording industry —
Addresses, essays, lectures. 2. Sound recordings — Addresses, essays, lectures. 3.
Music and society — Addresses, essays, lectures. 4. Mass media — Addresses,
essays, lectures. I. Blaukopf, Kurt. ML3795.P43 1983. 338.4′7789912. 82-16861.

ISBN 3-211-81725-5 Springer-Verlag Wien-New York
ISBN 0-387-81725-5 Springer-Verlag New York-Wien

Foreword

Since its creation, the International UNESCO-Fund for the Promotion of Culture has accorded particular attention to the problems of preserving and promoting music throughout the world.

Of the numerous initiatives launched with the Fund's support one ought to mention the foundation of an intercultural school of music in Venice; the fitting-out of a recording studio for the Music School of Jamaica; the collection of popular songs of the People's Republic of China; the organization of an experimental rostrum featuring films on traditional music and dance; the establishment of a music information centre for educational purposes; the launching of a music promotion service within the framework of the International Music Council; etc.

The present study, drawn up by the International Institute for Audio-Visual Communication and Cultural Development – MEDIACULT – belongs to the range of projects indicated above. Work on the study was directed by Professor Kurt Blaukopf and combined contributions by many researchers to a theme that had also been the subject of an international seminar held in Vienna, in November 1979.

We are glad that the Fund has been able to contribute to the realization and distribution of the study which is sure to facilitate a more exact definition of the complex and often new problems posed by the widespread use of recording equipment in all contemporary societies.

Felipe Herrera
President
of the Administrative Council,
International Fund
for the Promotion of Culture
of UNESCO

Contents

Wilhelm Schlemm
On the Position of the "Tonmeister" (Sound Recordist) in the Musical
Communication Process 151

Karl Breh
High Fidelity, Stereophony, and the Mutation of Musical Communication 165

Annex I
List of Experts Cooperating in the Project 179

Annex II
Contributions Made to the Project Not Contained in this Publication 181

Introduction

In May 1978, the International Fund for the Promotion of Culture of UNESCO decided to sponsor a project concerned with the role of the audio and audio-visual recordings in contemporary society. The individual tasks were:

1. to analyze the role of audio and audio-visual recordings in the cultural and economic statistics of some industrial countries;
2. to point out the major gaps in this field;
3. to formulate recommendations for a methodology applicable to the study of the phonographic industry.

In the solution of this task the collaboration of experts from the fields of statistics, sociology, acoustics, mass communication, phonographic industry, etc. was sought. [The names of these experts are listed in Annex I.]

The subject of the project was treated in 18 written contributions made by experts from 10 countries. The interdisciplinary approach, in addition, necessitated the organization of a seminar for the discussion of the results arrived at in individual papers.

The present publication, apart from 11 original contributions, also contains a methodological summary concerning statistics of culture [Paul Beaud] as well as a résumé of the conclusions arrived at with indications concerning the orientation of future research work in this field [Irmgard Bontinck]. When the project was in the planning stage, opinions on the value of such research were by no means unanimously in favour. At a later stage, however, it became obvious that not only experts but also cultural and communication policy makers in some countries had become sensitized, at least in part by the research initiatives of MEDIACULT. The value of such research as decision-making aid in cultural and communication policy is also reflected in the multiplying effect evidenced by research projects meanwhile taken up in various countries.

The work so far accomplished by MEDIACULT should be understood as a first stage. Follow-up projects may benefit both from the recommendations made and from the methodological synthesis. It ought to be duly emphasized that all previous studies have been restricted to industrial countries and that it has now become possible to expand research also to developing countries.

MEDIACULT is greatly indebted to the International Fund for the Promotion of Culture without whose assistance such broadly based, international research would have been impossible. My thanks are also due to the experts who participated in this venture. All those who took part in the project were agreed that this first stage could only mean one step in the desired direction, but that it provided the basis for follow-up research and international cooperation. This research is no end in itself [though its theoretical value is uncontested] but an effort to develop instruments facilitating decision-making in the fields of cultural and communication policy.

Kurt Blaukopf
Director MEDIACULT

Irmgard Bontinck

The Project: Aims and Results

In recent years, cultural sociology has repeatedly pointed to the fact that the technical media in general and the phonogram in particular have caused or at least initiated changes in socio-cultural processes and socio-musical structures. Pop, beat and rock are unthinkable without electro-acoustic manipulation. These musical genres have their primary existence not in live performance but in the production for or recording on phonograms. The new technologies have also invaded the sphere of so-called "serious" music, causing profound changes in production, communication and reception. Unlimited reproducibility, extended repertoire, increased accessibility, a quality of performance raised to perfection, vast expansion of the music market and manifold possibilities of obtaining information about music are but a few aspects of the massive penetration of music into social reality brought about by phonogram technology.

Cultural Change

This process has generated and still generates new variants of cultural communication. Most significant in quantitative terms is the so-called "second" way of cultural communication, namely technical communication which is gaining increasing importance in society. The immediate past, however, has been marked by a growing number of qualitative changes, which in their turn have repercussions on the traditional type of musical life. It is not only the habituating effect on listening expectations and listening experience that makes itself felt; research has also shown that the growing share of phonograms in musical communication is by no means bound to engender passive cultural behaviour. On the contrary, proof has been furnished that involvement in musical activities is steadily spreading not only in the sector of youth music, where a combination of musical and electro-acoustic instruments is employed, but also in conventional musical practice and in folk music.

Linked with economic, legal and technical aspects, the changes in cultural communication have also occasioned mutations of cultural life. The phonographic industry, radio and television authorities have become decisive factors in cultural life, musical policy is gaining importance within the cultural-policy frameworks of countries. The intertwining of conventional mechanisms of musical life with new administrative-technical and economic structures and operating mechanisms has created a situation in which cultural life is increasingly determined by factors defying definition.

Music

While MEDIACULT-research into the role of audio-visual communication in cultural development was in progress, the sector of musical communication gradually moved to the centre of attention. Numerous studies and the experience and findings derived from them lent increasing urgency to the task of investigating the role of phonograms in musical communication. All the more so, since previous work had revealed that the role of the phonogram in cultural development is imperfectly understood and comprehensive preparatory work had revealed that statistics and cultural research, cultural sociology and empirical social research have done very little to shed light on this issue, in other words, that there is hardly any reliable and comparable data available.

Data Collection

As the project progressed the following sectors were treated in a substantial number of studies: national statistical surveys covering the phonographic industry (data available about production, distribution, consumption), legal, economic and technical aspects of phonograms, findings of cultural research and cultural sociology related to the mutation of cultural behaviour through phonograms, cultural policy and musical policy, impact of the phonographic industry on the cultural policy of a country, role of phonograms in broadcasting, etc.

An Inter-Disciplinary Seminar

When the work listed in the project schedule had been concluded and the material gathered, MEDIACULT arranged an international seminar on "The Phonogram in Cultural Communication", which was held in Vienna, from November 12 – 14, 1979. Experts from diverse disciplines had been invited to take part in an exchange of opinions, with the aim of

1. ascertaining the availability of data on phonograms or spotting gaps in official statistics,

2. drawing up recommendations designed to serve as basis for the drafting of a methodology to be employed in inquiries into the phonographic industry.

The following disciplines were involved in the discussion of the research findings and of the above-mentioned issues:

Communication research
Cultural sociology
Statistics
Acoustics
Phonogram production and marketing
Musicology
Music psychology
Ethnomusicology
Radio and TV-programming
Copyright
Recording technique

In the course of the consultation the place value of the phonogram in the cultural and economic statistics of several industrial countries was outlined and the lack of relevant statistics revealed. The discussion of the role played by phonograms in contemporary life, tackling the issue from the angles of different disciplines, stimulated new projects dealing not only with the quantitative but also with the qualitative place value of the phonogram in cultural communication.

Preliminary Results

From the papers contained in the present volume as well as from additional contributions made to this project (see list Annex II) the following results can be derived:

1. To spot gaps in statistics should not be regarded as an aim in itself. What makes the lack of statistical information so particularly deplorable is the fact that crucial problems affecting cultural-policy making and cultural development are not provable, i.e. are not in statistical evidence.

2. The phonogram technology offers new possibilities of gaining access to and preserving cultural practice, particularly in developing countries.

3. Inherent in the adoption of these technologies is also a trend towards stereotypes which will not do justice to the variety of cultures based on oral tradition.

4. Phonograms as well as videograms can help to give access to culture especially in regions where such access would otherwise be limited for certain reasons, like transport facilities etc.

5. Phonograms and videograms can serve the presentation of the culture of one particular country or region to others and thereby contribute to a more balanced flow of cultural communication.

6. Dissimilarities in the access to culture also result from dissimilarities in the production of phonograms and videograms as well as in the field of distribution. Cultural-policy decisions ought to be based on precise data about the production and distribution of phonograms and videograms.

7. The recording of cultural messages on phonograms leads to what has been described as "discomorphosis", i.e.,

a) the adaptation of the creative process to technical conditions,

b) the qualitative change of the cultural message brought about by the specific mechanism of the recording process, and

c) a corresponding change in the reception of the cultural message.

8. Production, distribution and diffusion of phonograms have given rise to a number of new professions. In view of the importance of these new and more specialized activities it was found that a closer study of "career patterns" connected with phonograms should be undertaken. This applies to a certain extent also to videograms.

9. Cultural development has been found to depend to a high degree upon the development of phonograms and videograms. Thus, it seems imperative to include the study of the reception of phonograms into cultural research and statistics on culture.

Paul Beaud

Statistics and Methodology

One thing is to be pointed out at the very beginning: statistical methods of data collection should never be discussed without reference to their purpose. A neutral methodology does not exist: the statistical measuring instruments to be dealt with in the following must always serve the solution of certain problems encountered either by those involved in research or by those responsible for the formulation or implementation of a cultural policy.

Today, social scientists as well as all those concerned with cultural activities at different levels are faced with a central problem: the growing internationalization of the cultural industry with its qualitative and quantitative aspects. It may well be that no other sector of this industry has reached a degree of international concentration comparable to that of the record industry. At present, five record companies account for 60% of all sales in the industrialized, capitalist countries: three North American ones, a British one and a German-Dutch one. Such concentration is encountered vertically and horizontally, as it extends to the manufacturing of reproduction equipment and to distribution, which are often dominated by the same multinational companies.

The cultural industry, once a light industry dominated by individual know-how, has developed into a heavy industry whose survival depends on its success in international markets on account of the enormous investments involved. Thus, an entirely new logic of production has developed in a sector where a certain form of industrial craftsmanship used to play an important role before its existence came to be threatened by concentration. This is a fundamental new fact which has to be taken into consideration in any study concerned with the record. Several participants of the Vienna seminar were able to quantify the market shares held by multinationals in their respective countries. As the figures can be seen from their contributions[1], this report will be limited to a discussion of the new problems and questions resulting from this internationalization at three levels: production, distribution, consumption. The usefulness of a statistical instrument from the viewpoint of cultural policy largely depends on whether it permits quantitative and qualitative comparisons of the development of national production with that of multinational companies and an evaluation of the resulting modifications in the structure of consumption, as has been shown by the Swedish and Canadian studies.

To begin with, an attempt will be made to identify the deficiencies of existing statistical material; then, some categories and typologies, permitting national and international comparisons at the three above-mentioned levels, will be suggested. The problem of access to existing data and that of improved coordination of research methods will also be referred to.

1. The Deficiencies of Statistics

In view of the enormous differences from country to country, the deficiencies of statistical material on phonograms are difficult to illustrate on a global basis. Sometimes, even the most elementary economic data are either not available or have never been presented in a matter as to permit their utilization for our purposes.

Nevertheless, two major categories of quantitative and qualitative data can be identified, which have never been compiled in a satisfactory manner: data on the development of mutual international influences and data on individual consumption.

Whereas other markets, such as that of the cinema, the publishing industry and television, have already been studied on a worldwide basis and have been the subject of regular publications for several years, information on the record market is still insufficient, although the process of concentration is more advanced there than in other markets and extends to almost all capitalist countries, irrespective of their degree of economic development, a tendency which is far less pronounced in other sectors of the cultural industry.

The internationalization of the phonogram industry has to be analyzed at several levels. Let us begin at the macro-economic level. As far as we know, there is a single preliminary study attempting to collect all statistical information made available by private industry itself and dealing with the

---

[1] Cf. in particular, the contributions by Del Grosso Destreri, Luigi and Corposanto, Cleto, [p. 79], Ferland, Yvon and Anderson, Robert D. [p. 19], Malm, Krister [p. 43] and Signitzer, Benno and Wallnöfer, Pierre [p. 133].

major phonogram producers all over the world[2]. In particular, the study draws attention to the recent appearance of new forms of production and distribution and to another phenomenon, little known as yet – the existence of companies specializing in the production of albums consisting of "hits" previously recorded by other companies and now available on records which are intensively advertised on radio and television.

These companies spend up to one third of their turnover on sales promotion and operate on the basis of non-conventional distribution networks. In Austria, two companies of this type[3] accounted for 15% of all domestic sales in 1978, as compared to no more than 2% in 1976[4], thus forcing the multinational companies to apply the same methods.

This example illustrates the importance of approaching production both from the quantitative (development of international currents, position of national producers) and from the qualitative point of view. The concentration of production and distribution (development of sales through "rack-jobbing") reflects a change in the structure of the market and the concentration of sales on a small number of titles. This development is quite obvious in "disco" music. Yet, it is no less significant in other genres. Hennion and Vignolle[5] have shown that the domination of the French classical music market by the multinationals has been accompanied by the gradual disappearance of certain national schools, which do not easily lend themselves to international distribution in the opinion of these companies. On the other hand, the strategy of the multinationals themselves with regard to artistic contents is profoundly influenced by the necessity to penetrate various national markets and to produce commodities based on archetypes, which sell easily in different cultural contexts as long as they are simple and unrefined.

Understanding this mechanism and its effects on the musical supply situation requires a profound knowledge of the development of recordings and sales of works from an extended historical period, both with regard to works protected by copyright and others which have become public property. Again, as far as we know, not a single systematic study of this kind dealing with quantitative, qualitative, economic, sociological or musicological aspects has been undertaken so far.

As mentioned above, the second "white spot" of our knowledge of the musical market is individual consumption. Rarely has it been the

---

[2] Cf. Soramäki, Martti and Haarma, Sukka, The International Music Industry, The Finnish Broadcasting Company, Planning and Research Department, Helsinki 1978.

[3] An American and an English one.

[4] Cf. the contribution by Signitzer, Benno and Wallnöfer, Pierre [p. 133].

[5] Hennion, Antoine, and Vignolle, Jean-Pierre, Artisans et Industriels du Disque, CSI/CORDES, Paris 1978, 332 pages, mimeogr.

subject of detailed, specific studies, and most of the figures available have been derived from general studies on cultural practices in which the record holds no more than a marginal position in relation to other cultural activities, considered to be more important, on the one hand and the principal mass communication media – cinema, press, radio and, above all, television – on the other hand.

The few figures available are based on rough classifications both with regard to the musical and the socio-professional categories serving as a basis for the investigation of samples. This problem will again be referred to later on. For the time being, an example – already quoted in an earlier paper[6] – is to be sufficient. Having studied the available statistics on musical consumption in France since 1960 from the viewpoint of a future historian of these two decades, we found that the latter would not come across any indication of the existence of profound cultural movements, particularly among the contemporary youth, which were dialectically linked to the enormous distribution of new musical genres.

When talking about cultural statistics, it is certainly no mistake to expect them to take account of a development which profoundly affects existing value systems. A micro-analytical approach, e.g. centred on specific audiences or particular cultural "events", does not exclude quantification. On the contrary, abstaining from the approximations which by necessity result from repeated efforts to grasp the totality of cultural practices of extremely varied populations very often opens up the possibility to quantify qualitative aspects, to create comparable categories on the basis of similar samples and coherent problems common to scientists of different countries.

2. Categories and Typologies

Both at the national and at the international level, the exploitation and the comparability of statistical data depend on the adoption of stable and precise categories and typologies. Conditions which are hardly ever fulfilled: the socio-professional categories used in opinion surveys vary from country to country and in the field of music certain terms turn out to be untranslatable or apply to different realities (in France, for example, the term "pop music" does not have the same meaning as in its country of origin). Any international comparison must be based on

– the adoption of similar basic variables with regard to the collection of economic data,

---

[6] Cf. Beaud, Paul, Methodologische Probleme. In: Blaukopf, Kurt, Massenmedium Schallplatte, Breitkopf und Härtel, Wiesbaden 1977, pp. 66 – 87.

- the selection of comparable social indicators concerning the populations to be studied,
- a standardization of the musical categories used.

Recent studies carried out in France[7] and Canada[8] may serve as a methodological basis for the collection and presentation of economic data on the phonographic industry in accordance with the traditional division: production, distribution, individual consumption.

a) Production

It goes without saying that the record and the magnetic tape do not exist in isolation from the reproduction equipment permitting their utilization. The need to take account of the manufacturing of reproduction equipment is the more obvious, as this is a sector of industry in which technological choices have and will have an important impact on artistic contents and which has been characterized by tough international competition ever since the arrival of "hardware" producer (e.g. Japan) in a market which used to be dominated by multinational companies producing both "hardware" and "software".

For each individual country the development of production has to be examined on the basis of three main criteria: value, quantities, and numbers of titles and their circulation.

Production in terms of value — imports/exports
- Overall turnover of the phonographic industry
- Overall turnover of the reproduction equipment industry
- Number of companies — classification of companies according to their capital structure (national, mixed, foreign)
- Labour force employed in the various fields
- Value of domestic production (records, tapes, reproduction equipment, etc.)
- Value of imports and exports of the various fields
- Trade balance in terms of value
- Domestic market, imports and exports in terms of value according to supports (format, replay speed, etc.)
- Domestic market, imports and exports in terms of value according to types of reproduction equipment
- Production costs, analytical book-keeping for every production
- Consumer price index for records, unrecorded and recorded magnetic tapes and electronic material

---

[7] Cf. Hennion, Antoine, and Vignolle, Jean-Pierre, op. cit.
[8] Cf. the contribution by Ferland, Yvon, and Anderson, Robert D. [p. 19].

— Royalties paid (at home and abroad).

Production in terms of quantity
— Quantities manufactured according to supports, formats, types of equipment
— Corresponding figures for imports and exports
— Quantities sold (same apportionment)
— Quantities sold according to genres.

Production in terms of numbers of titles and circulation
     As far as production is concerned, this is the most significant element, as it provides information on the qualitative development of production and the changes of the musical offer resulting from the economic transformations of the entire sector.

— Number of titles produced according to supports, formats, genres
— Origin of titles (national, foreign)
— New editions and re-editions
— Average circulation according to formats and genres.

b) Distribution

     The development of the sales structure according to different distribution networks is a particularly important indicator of the qualitative development of production and the consumption of phonograms. In fact, the specialization of distribution networks corresponds to more and more highly differenciated selling strategies and artistic options[9].

     To begin with, the approach to this sector consists of the collection of general economic data on the number of companies, their turnover, potential fields of specialization, their links with the phonographic and electronic industries. Then, an attempt will be made to differentiate retail sales (volume, genres) according to points of sale. Thus, the following categories will be obtained:

— Number of distributors, classified according to types (editors, wholesalers, rack-jobbers) — capital structure — turnover — percentages of the national market

---

[9] Here is a most striking example of the importance of this sector: Krister Malm has shown that in spite of the continuous increase of phonogram sales in the seventies, the number of works offered to the Swedish public has decreased. The new distribution systems, mainly rack-jobbing, call for rapid stock rotation and a sales policy based on the quick succession of a small number of ephemeral successes and many points of sales [petrol stations, super-markets, etc.], staffed by non-specialized personnel who are not able to supply customers with any information on the recordings other than that on the record sleeves [cf. p. 63].

- Number of points of sale
- Classification of points of sale: record stores, department stores with a specialized department, rack-shops
- Classification of sales (volume, value, formats, genres) according to the different distribution networks.

c) Consumption

The consumption of phonograms can be considered at three different levels: collective (radio, television, dance-clubs, etc.), semi-collective (record libraries) and individual (purchases by individuals). The collective level can be approached in two ways: either through statistics on the receipt of royalties made available by the national bodies in charge of their collection, or through the data of radio and television organizations on the annual number of hours of music broadcasts according to genres.

However, international comparisons of such figures have turned out to be rather dubious. Royalties vary according to national agreements. Radio and television statistics do not always distinguish between recorded music and live broadcasts. Therefore, it is desirable to emphasize the improvement of data collection on semi-collective and individual consumption.

Borrowings from record libraries

Making use of the index cards of public and semi-public record libraries, which contain some basic information on the subscribers (age, sex, occupation), may be a substitute for time-consuming studies on consumption by individuals. These analyses might permit the collection of very precise qualitative information on borrowings according to socio-demographic categories.

The following statistical data would be most easily available:
- Classification of record libraries according to their origin
- Inventory of the libraries, by format, by genre, by value
- Borrowings:
  - . number of borrowers
  - . apportionment according to the available socio-demographic categories
  - . apportionment of borrowings according to these categories and according to genres.

Consumption by individuals

Sociologically and from the viewpoint of cultural policy, this is one of the most important sectors. In most countries, it is also the sector on which the least information is available. This section should contain general data on the equipment of households on the one hand and qualitative date on the habits of the users of such equipment on the other hand.

General data
— Households equipped with: record-players, stereo equipment, cassette and tape recorders
— Numbers of records, cassettes and tapes (unrecorded or recorded) per household
— Annual budget for the purchase of records, cassettes, tapes and reproduction equipment.

Comparisons with other equipments and other budget items under the heading "leisure time and cultural activities" would be helpful.

Specific data
A first effort has to be made to standardize the socio-demographic and, above all, the musical categories used for the collection and presentation of statistical material.

The collection of data should be approached along two main lines: semi-qualitative studies on consumption and the listening habits of the population in general and micro-sociological research on specific audiences (the young public, for example, which is known to be the largest group of consumers of recorded music) or on extraordinary "musical events" (e.g. the sudden success of a record of a genre which is not normally suited for mass distribution). We are not going to list the whole range of variables to be taken into consideration in a quantitative and quantifiable approach to the cultural habits of individuals, as it is bound to be tedious and would always be incomplete and untranslatable from one context to another. For our purposes, it is most important to understand the social logic of the formation and development of hierarchies, habits and musical tastes through studies relating both to the purchase of phonograms (motivations, genres, places of purchase, etc.) and their utilization (frequency, "service life" according to genres, etc.), in connection with their relationships to the socio-demographic data and the musical and — in a wider context — even the cultural habits of the populations concerned.

3. Access to Data

The creation of a statistical instrument according to the categories defined above first of all calls for the compilation of existing, though widely dispersed, data. At the very beginning, it should be pointed out that problems concerning the access to sources of information (authorities, professional associations, industry, etc.) seem to differ greatly from country to country. In the Socialist countries[10] information on overall production, the distribution of sales by titles or the nature of international exchanges can be obtained quite easily. In countries with a free market economy some of these data are regarded as business or fiscal secrets and sometimes even public authorities surround themselves with an air of secrecy.

In general, there are three sources of statistical material on phonograms: official sources, statistics of institutions and empirical studies carried out at universities, by industry or by public authorities.

a) Official Statistics

Usually, official statistics provide macro-economic information of the most general nature. Ministerial departments in charge of the supervision of industry and foreign trade make available detailed information, both in terms of quantity and in terms of value, on national production and on imports and exports of phonograms as well as reproduction equipment. However, very often these data are purely economic in nature and do not furnish any qualitative information on the products in question.

If dépôt légal is provided for under the country's copyright legislation, the development of national production can be followed up according to formats and musical genres. For example, the Phonothèque Nationale Française[11] registers all new records, cassettes, cartridges, magnetic tapes and video tapes every year and classifies the phonograms deposited according to musical genres. Yet, such information reflects the development of the market in a very distorted manner, as there may be considerable variations of sales according to formats and musical genres.

b) Statistics of Institutions

This approach to the phonogram market is of a more qualitative nature and rests on data provided mainly by private industry and its professional associations and organizations in charge of the collection of royalties and fees for mechanical reproduction.

In fact, it is through these bodies that information on sales according to genres and even according to titles and distribution networks can be obtained, as the copyright societies apportion the amounts received according to places or means of collective distribution.

As mentioned above, record libraries are a potential source of accurate qualitative information on consumption by individuals as yet largely

---

[10] Cf. the contribution by Sági, Mária [p. 111].

[11] Cf. Hennion, Antoine, and Vignolle, Jean-Pierre, op. cit.

unexploited. The trade associations of record sellers can also be contacted (such cooperation has already been initiated between UNESCO and the trade associations of booksellers). Radio and television organizations normally compile statistics on the number of hours devoted to music broadcasts. Frequently, they also carry out opinion polls to obtain some information on the musical tastes of their listeners. This will again be referred to later on.

As mentioned above, one of the major problems of a cultural policy in this field is to arrive at an accurate understanding of the economic development of this sector and the effects of the growing international-ization of the phonographic industry on national production, both with regard to qualitative and quantitative aspects.

This understanding must be based on the cooperation of industry itself in the collection of economic and even musicological data. The very detailed results obtained by Canadian scientists[12] from questionnaires sent to all national record producers show that such cooperation is possible today. In particular, the study precisely reveals the origin not only of the capital of these companies but also of their musical productions.

c) Empirical Research

Information on musical consumption and on the development of the relationships between supply and demand is mainly obtained through empirical research of different origin. A small but growing number of studies in this field is being undertaken by members of the academic community all over the world. In view of the small number of studies available, their degree of specialization and the existence of an exchange network among scientists, it should not be too difficult to survey research work already completed or in progress.

Sometimes, empirical studies on musical production and consumption are also undertaken by public bodies (ministries in charge of cultural affairs, national radio and television organizations). And finally, although the representatives of industry themselves insist that market studies are impossible in a field in which success is unpredictable and only depends on the subjectivity of the public, such studies do exist and may prove to be a valuable help in understanding the development of musical tastes. The understandable reluctance of industry to disclose the results can be overcome, as there is a certain reciprocity in the disclosure and circulation of such information and centralized statistics of this kind have proved to be a useful instrument.

---

[12] Cf. the contribution by Ferland, Yvon, and Anderson, Robert D. [p. 19].

4. The Harmonization of Different Types of Research and Their Methodologies

As can be seen from the above said, some of the tasks outlined call for the coordination and centralization of data collected at the national level by bodies often unknown to each other and of research undertaken in different countries without any possibility of comparing the results, which is often due to nothing else but a lack of common methods and a common terminology.

However, our understanding of cultural phenomena should not be limited to the macro-economic approach: even when looked upon as a commodity, music still conveys a meaning of its own. The cultural impact of the structural transformations of the musical industry cannot possibly be grasped without multi-disciplinary cooperation of economists, sociologists, musicologists and professional representatives of other industrial, technical and artistic sectors.

If these different approaches to the problem are to complement — if not to meet — each other, and if the efficiency of research is to be increased, a first effort to harmonize existing methodologies has to be made at the four levels of any empirical research: collection of data, classification, processing and storage; such effort calls for the standardization of social indicators and musical typologies. The present report is intended to provide a preliminary basis for discussions along these lines, a methodological framework which may serve all those who are interested in this field to varying degrees.

Yvon Ferland and Robert D. Anderson

The Recording Industry Survey Conducted in Canada

This report will describe our project on recording industry statistics.

First, we will view the project within the Program of Culture Statistics, then we will briefly touch the statistical information we already have on music and lastly, we will describe the specific project.

The Project as Part of the Program

The project is part of a much wider program to gather statistical information on all aspects of Canadian culture. Thus, to better understand the actual project, we thought it important to say a few words about the program.

For the last five years, Statistics Canada, with the cooperation of the Secretary of State Department responsible for cultural development at the federal level, has organized a comprehensive and integrated program of gathering and analyzing statistics on culture. It covers cultural institutions, cultural industries and cultural activities of Canadians either as artists or as users of cultural goods and services.

We have obtained statistical information on records and tapes indirectly through our surveys of activities of Canadians and cultural institutions. But, it is mostly through cultural industry surveys that the recording industry information is collected.

We have identified six main cultural industries, namely, book publishing, film, periodicals, performing arts, electronic media, and finally, audio recording.

For each one, we want to know about their structural organization, their links with similar industries, their financial situation, the type of personnel they employ and the main characteristics of their manufactured cultural goods. Two specific aspects are of great interest to us. First, we want to measure the importance of *Canadian* production of cultural goods relative to the total Canadian consumption and secondly, examine the extent to which Canadian production represents our culture in its content and even its form.

These general objectives apply to the recording industry as well. Let us now turn briefly to the information available on music.

Music in Canada

We already have a good stock of statistical information on music in Canada. We are still lacking in some areas but we intend to correct this in the near future.

We examined a series of consumer activities relating to music and gathered information on attendance to operas, classical concerts, popular music performances and ballets. We asked Canadians, in 1972, 1975 and 1978, about record and tape listening at home. We also have statistics on radio listening by program and television watching. We know who is interested in music in Canada, what kind of music they are interested in, the way they listen to it, the time they spend listening and the money they spend on equipment and concerts.

We collected a substantial amount of data on performances and music companies or groups but still lack information on composers and music performers. We intend to fill this gap during the next few years. Indeed, we have an ongoing project on creative and performing artists. Last year, we surveyed painters and sculptors in the framework of the project. This year, we are surveying writers and plan to do the same for performers and other artistic groups.

Because a large portion of music is heard through radio and television, we have collected statistical data on these programs. We know what programs are being offered to the public and what time they are broadcast.

For the first time in 1978, we conducted a survey on the recording industry. We had been partly deficient in this area.

The Project Itself

The first step in preparation for organizing the survey of the record industry was to consult with members of the various sectors of the industry and those government departments and agencies which by virtue of their mandates would be interested in the industry's performance. It was through these consultations that the objectives of the survey, the identification of the potential users and the identification of the re-spondents were made.

The objectives mentioned above for any cultural industry were also valid here. Furthermore, we specifically tried to determine the main activities of record companies, the origin and content of record production and the revenues and expenditures involved in this activity, along with the revenues earned from industry-related activities such as sales of rights.

The users of this information were identified as (1) those federal and provincial government departments and agencies concerned with industrial development, the production of artists, cultural policy, and the effects of the laws of copyright as they apply to the sound recording industry; (2) the various recording industry associations which wanted to monitor the state of the industry in general; (3) individual record companies which wanted to gauge their production and revenues in relation to the industry as a whole; and (4) the trade media and university departments of media studies.

The respondents to the survey were indicated by the manner in which we defined the unit of analysis – those companies which released sound recordings either from master tapes produced by the reporting company itself or from master tapes leased from other companies, and, those companies which produced master tapes and licenced the right to manufacture sound recordings to other companies. The actual names of the companies were gathered from industry association membership lists and since this survey was envisioned as a census of all record companies the trade publications were researched for other companies.

The preparation of the survey documents themselves required a series of meetings with industry personnel. At these meetings the respondents' ability to supply the information was assessed. We also explained to the respondents the benefits they could derive from the statistical information. A pilot survey was carried out on a sample of companies picked according to size of gross revenue, type of production, and language of operation.

The survey documents themselves were written in a neutral, technical language utilizing the terminology and phraseology of the industry but avoiding any inconsistent jargon.

This whole process of consultation was started in the fall of 1976. The first draft of the questionnaire for the presentation to the industry for their comments was completed in April 1977. The first compilation of a list of possible respondents was also completed for presentation to the industry associations. An extensive round of meetings was held in April and May 1977 for this purpose. It was followed by a major revision of the questionnaire and by the preparation of the instruction booklet. On June 2, 1977, at a meeting of a working committee, it was decided that the documents were ready for a pre-test. Consequently, for this pre-test, 13 companies were picked by language of production, type of company and estimated volume of business.

The pre-test indicated that (1) the questionnaire contained far too many questions; (2) that there was a problem of double-reporting. Thus another version simplified both substantially and put in logical order was completed in October 1977. Copies were again sent to the associations and the final version was completed December 14, 1977.

Two hundred and four questionnaires were mailed out on June 1, 1978 and a telephone follow-up started shortly thereafter. It was expected that many of the companies receiving the questionnaires might not be record companies as we defined them. Of the 204 questionnaires sent out, 74 of those returned were considered to be within our definition of a record company. Approximately 10 companies which indicated during the telephone follow-up that they were record companies and would be returning the questionnaire did not in fact do so. The remaining questionnaires were either returned by the post-office as undeliverable or were returned by companies which were not, in fact, record companies. We estimate that companies which should have reported but did not in fact do so were responsible for sales of approximately 1% of the total industry sales. This estimate is based on quotations gathered from the non-reporting companies themselves during a second follow-up.

Respondents did not note any specific difficulties in answering the questionnaire and no problems were really expected since we had done a pilot test. What did vary from company to company was the completeness of their own file-keeping systems which in effect determined how much work was involved in actually gathering together the information to fill out the questionnaires. On some occasions the respondents did not want to provide a detailed breakdown of the sources of their revenue and had to be re-assured that their specific questionnaires were strictly confidential. It is assumed that these above difficulties have been more or less overcome now since the companies have had a go at the task.

Countries that have a method of identifying record releases by local musicians could easily adapt this questionnaire to their own particular situation. The only question that may not be applicable to the situation in other countries would be the last question dealing with the amount of manufacturer's sales tax paid. All other questions could easily be written to reflect the local situation. Those countries that have an artist's royalty in the copyright of the sound recording itself (which is not the case in Canada) could modify Question 23 to include this form of royalty.

A copy of the exact questionnaire used follows as well as the instruction booklet.

Questionnaire

Statistics   Statistique
Canada   Canada
Education, Science & Culture Division
Arts and Media Section

Confidential
(when completed)

6540 A

Authority — Statistics Acts,
Chapter 15, Statutes of
Canada 1970-71-72.

SURVEY OF THE RECORDING INDUSTRY 1977

Please refer to the Instruction Booklet before completing the questionnaire.
Please answer all questions unless instructed to skip. If the answer to a particular question is zero, indicate by a "0" in the appropriate box, if not available or unknown enter a "U".
Please return this Questionnaire within 60 days of receipt of this request.

This questionnaire is to be completed by your Canadian head office. If this address is branch office, please indicate the name and postal address of your Canadian head office and return the questionnaire in the envelope provided.

Name of Canadian head office	Postal address

ELIGIBILITY TO REPORT

Did this organization release records (see definition in instruction booklet) from masters which were either owned by this organization or leased from another organization during the reporting period?

001 | 2 ☐ No   1 ☐ Yes

Did this organization lease or sell a master tape to another organization during the reporting period for the release of discs or tapes by them?

002 | 2 ☐ No   1 ☐ Yes — to an organization in Canada. Please list the names of all such companies. (separate sheet may be used if needed)

003 | 1 ☐ Yes — to an organization in another country.

(if you have answered "No" to both questions 1 and 2, you are not required to report. Please indicate briefly the nature of your business and then return this questionnaire in the envelope provided so that we may remove your name from our mailing list — Thank you for your co-operation.)

PRELIMINARY DESCRIPTION OF REPORTING ORGANIZATION

Indicate the starting and ending dates for your last complete financial year ending at any time between April 1, 1977 and March 31, 1978 inclusive.

From:	Day	Month	Year
To:	Day	Month	Year

3. Indicate the number of branch offices and the number of employees of this organization

Branches	004
Employees	005

4. Is this organization a subsidiary of another organization (check one box only)

006 1 ☐ No
    2 ☐ Yes, with head office of parent company located in Canada
          Name————————————————————————————
    3 ☐ Yes, with head office of parent company located outside
       Canada
          Name————————————————————————————

5. Indicate the country in which the controlling interest of this organization is located (check one box only)

007 1 ☐ Canada 2 ☐ United States 3 ☐ other (specify) ——————

6. Indicate the category of the legal status of this organization (check one box only)

008 1 ☐ Sole proprietorship   2 ☐ Partnership   3 ☐ Co-operative
    4 ☐ Incorporated organization 5 ☐ Incorporated organization for
       not for profit   profit – public
    6 ☐ Incorporated organization 7 ☐ Other (specify) ——————
       for profit – private

7. Indicate how long this organization has been established in Canada

009 1 ☐ Less than two years   2 ☐ Two to five years
    3 ☐ Six to ten years   4 ☐ Over ten years

RELEASES

Questions 8 to 19 are to be answered only by those organizations which released records (i.e. answered "Yes" to question 1). Others proceed directly to question 20.

8. Did this organization release records during the reporting period from a master which was:

		Yes	No
1. Produced by this organization	020	1 ☐	2 ☐
2. Leased or bought from an organization located within Canada	021	1 ☐	2 ☐
3. Leased or bought from an organization located in another country	022	1 ☐	2 ☐

9. Please list the names of all organizations located in Canada from which your organization leased (or bought) masters during the reporting period. (A separate sheet may be attached if necessary.)

_____

_____

_____

10. Did this organization also distribute discs or tapes (not the leasing of masters) on an exclusive territorial basis for other organizations during the reporting period?

030 1 ☐ Yes   2 ☐ No (proceed to question 12)

11. Please list the names of all organizations located in Canada for which you distributed discs or tapes (A separate sheet may be attached if necessary).

_____

_____

_____

12. Indicate the number of releases (not quantity of discs pressed) according to the origin of the master and the format of manufacture.

	Format of Manufacture	
	7″ Disc	12″ Disc
Master:		
1. Produced by this organization		
2. Leased or bought from another organization located in Canada		
3. Leased or bought from an organization in a foreign country		
Total number of releases		

13. Indicate the number of releases according to the number of Canadian content releases and the origin of the master.

	Releases containing at least one Canadian content selection		All other releases	
	7″ Disc	12″ Disc or tape	7″ Disc	12″ Disc or tape[1]
Master: 1. Produced by this organization	070	080	090	100
2. Leased or bought from another organization located in Canada	071	081	091	101
3. Leased or bought from an organization in a foreign country	072	082	092	102
Total	073	083	093	103

14. Indicate the number of releases by musical category and Canadian content.

	Releases containing at least one Canadian content selection		All other releases	
	7″ Disc	12″ Disc or tape	7″ Disc	12″ Disc or tape[1]
1. Adult-oriented popular music	200	210	220	230
2. Top 40 or rock-oriented music	201	211	221	231
3. Classical	202	212	222	232
4. Jazz	203	213	223	233
5. Country and folk	204	214	224	234
6. Children's	205	215	225	235

[1] If a record is released in both a disc and tape format, count it only once.

	Releases containing at least one Canadian content selection		All other releases	
	7" Disc	12" Disc or tape	7" Disc	12" Disc or tape[1]
7. Other	206	216	226	236
Total	207	217	227	237

15. Indicate the number of releases by language of lyrics and Canadian content.

	Releases containing at least one Canadian content selection		All other releases	
	7" Disc	12" Disc or tape	7" Disc	12" Disc or tape[1]
1. English	300	310	320	330
2. French	301	311	321	331
3. Both French and English	302	312	322	332
4. Other languages	303	313	323	333
5. No lyrics	304	314	324	334
Total	305	315	325	335

[1] If a record is released in both a disc and tape format, count it only once.

16. Indicate the number of acts produced by your organization that had a release by your organization	400
17. Indicate the number of acts produced by your organization that had material released in another territory	410
18. Indicate the number of acts that had a release by your organization from a master leased from another organization located in Canada	420

REVENUE

19. Indicate your net sales of discs and tapes released by your company during the last financial year according to the origin of the master.

Master:	Domestic sales $ (omit cents)	Export sales $ (omit cents)
1. Produced by this organization	500	510
2. Leased or bought from another organization located in Canada	501	511
3. Leased or bought from an organization in a foreign country	502	512
Total	503	513

20. This question is to be answered only by those which either leased or sold masters to other organizations (i.e. answered yes to question 2).
    Indicate the total revenue which your organization received during your last financial year from the leasing or selling of masters to other organizations.

	$ (omit cents)
1. From organizations in Canada	520
2. From organizations in another country	521
Total	522

21. Indicate if this organization had any revenue during your last financial year from any of the following activities by checking ($\sqrt{}$) that activity and providing the *total revenue* for all activities checked:

1. Music publizing   600 ☐
2. Renting of studio time to others   601 ☐
3. Laquer mastering for others   602 ☐
4. Custom disc pressing   603 ☐
5. Custom tape duplicating   604 ☐
6. Jacket fabrication or design for others   605 ☐
7. Wholesale distribution for others   606 ☐
8. Rack-jobbing operation   607 ☐
9. Retail sales through record stores owned by this
   organization   608 ☐
10. Other retail sales, i.e. mail order, record club   609 ☐
11. Artist management or concert promotion and booking
    activities   610 ☐

Total gross revenue (net of taxes collected from
customers) for activities checked   620 $ (omit cents)

EXPENSES

22. Indicate total recording cost during last financial year. Include costs for only those masters for which your organization owns copyright in the original sound recording. (See instruction booklet)

1. Recording costs in Canada	630
2. Recording costs in another country	631
Total	633

23. Only those organizations which answered "yes" to question 1 are to complete this question. Indicate expenses on masters incurred during last financial year.

	Masters owned by reporting organization	Masters leased from organization in Canada	Masters leased from organization outside Canada
1. Mechanical royalties	650 $ (omit cents)	660 $ (omit cents)	670 $ (omit cents)
2. Lease fees and advances paid including AF of M fees	651	661	671
Total	652	662	672

24. Only those organizations which answered "Yes" to question 1 are to complete this question. Indicate total disc and tape manufacturing costs (including jackets) for records manufactured from masters owned by or leased by this organization. Indicate these costs for your last financial year.

1. Manufacturing costs in Canada	700 $ (omit cents)
2. Manufacturing costs outside Canada	701
Total	703

25. Indicate the amount your organization paid to advertise its records or acts during your last financial year

	In Canada $ (omit cents)	Outside Canada $ (omit cents)
1. Paid to publishers of print media: Trade publications	710	720
Consumer publications	711	721
2. Paid to television stations for consumer advertising	712	722
3. Paid to radio stations for consumers advertising	713	723

26. Indicate the amount of federal tax paid on the net sales of disc and tapes released by your organization during your last financial year	750 $ (omit cents)

Instruction Booklet

Introduction

This booklet has been developed as an integral part of the survey of record companies. It explains the scope and nature of the survey, the confidentiality of individual returns, the policy of non-disclosure in publications, the concepts and definitions used throughout the questionnaire, and gives instructions for answering individual questions.

This survey is one of a number being conducted concerning the various cultural industries in Canada. The results of the survey will be used by various governmental departments as an aid in the formulation of policies concerning the cultural industries. The industry itself has expressed on numerous occasions the view that there has been a general lack of awareness of the record industry among government departments and the financial community. Thus, this survey is intended to provide the kinds of information necessary for government departments to formulate policies concerning the record industry and therefore to help the industry itself.

Return your completed questionnaire *within 60 days* of receipt in the envelope provided. Additional questionnaires will be sent upon request. Keep at least one copy for your own files, and in the event that you encounter any difficulties, contact the Arts and Media Section of Statistics Canada at (613) 593-6862.

Scope and Nature of the Survey

This is a survey of two types of activities engaged in by the recording industry – the manufacture (i.e. release) of records and the production of master tapes. The object of this survey is to determine the quantity and content of record releases from record manufacturers and the trade in master tapes between production companies and record companies on a calendar year basis. A parallel object of this survey is to determine some selected expenses and revenues concerning the two activities being surveyed on a financial year basis.

Confidentiality of individual returns and confidentiality in publication

Survey results disseminated in any form, whether through ordinary Statistics Canada publications or by request from outside users are never released in such a form that would allow either the direct or indirect disclosure of any individual company's contribution to the volume or value of any production or financial statistic. The only people who see individual, completed questionnaires are employees of Statistics Canada who have taken an oath of secrecy to ensure that all individual survey information remains strictly confidential. No other individual, government agency or department or private organization has access to your individual questionnaire.

Records excluded from this survey

Any record not available for purchase by the general public.

Concepts and Definitions Used in the Survey

Reporting organization

This is the corporate entity identified by your company name. Under no circumstances should a Canadian subsidiary of a foreign record company consider the parent company to be the reporting organization.

A Master

An original sound recording or any generation of an original sound recording used in the manufacture of records. Usually this is a master tape.

To produce a master

To take the financial risk involved in creating an original sound recording and to have proprietary and copyright claim in the resulting sound recording. To produce a master implies recording costs.

To lease a master

To permit another company to manufacture discs or tapes from an original sound recording protected by copyright. To lease a master implies that the owners (or their agents) receive a fee from the manufacturing company.

To release a record

To arrange for the pressing of discs or the duplication of tapes in either your company owned facilities or by a custom pressing arrangement with a pressing plant. To release a record is also to be responsible for payment of the 12% federal sales tax assessed by Revenue Canada on sale of the finished product.

Canadian content (*CRTC values*)

A musical selection is deemed to be a Canadian content selection if it qualifies under any *two* of the following conditions:

(A) The instrumentation or lyrics were principally performed by a Canadian

(B) The music was composed by a Canadian

(C) The lyrics were written by a Canadian, and

(D) The live performance was wholly recorded in Canada.

Guide to Questionnaire

Reporting period: Questions 1 and 2:   During the calendar year 1977.
        Questions 3 to 7:   As of the last day of your last complete financial year ending at anytime between April 1, 1977 and March 31, 1978.
        Questions 8 to 18:   During the calendar year 1977.
        Questions 19 to 26:   During your last complete financial year ending at anytime between April 1, 1977 and March 31, 1978.

For any particular question, if you have nothing to report, enter "0"; if not available or unknown enter "U".

Question 2

Any arrangement whereby the owners (or their agents) of a master permit a record company to manufacture records is referred to as a "lease" in the survey.

How to proceed once you have answered Questions 1 and 2

Fill out the dates of your financial year *ending* at anytime between April 1, 1977 and March 31, 1978 inclusive.

All respondents answer Questions 3 to 7, 21, and 25; then

(1) If your company *leased masters* to other companies but did not *release* records itself answer Questions 20 and 22 only.

(2) If your company *released* records answer Questions 8 to 19, 22, 23, 24 and 26.

(3) If your company both *leased masters to others* and *released some records itself*, then report your *leasing* activity in Question 20 and your *releasing* activity in Questions 8 to 19, 22, 23, 24 and 26.

Question 3

Do *not* include the head office in your count of branch offices. A "branch office" would be under the control of your Canadian head office. The total number of employees refers to all those who work for your head office and any branch offices in any country.

Question 4

If it should happen that your organization is a subsidiary of a company whose head office is located in Canada but is in turn a subsidiary of a parent company whose head office is located outside of Canada, then indicate that you are a subsidiary of a company with head office located outside of Canada.

Question 5

"Controlling interest" is the ability or potential ability of an individual, a group of individuals or a company to determine the operating and financial policies of the reporting organization including the ability to select the majority of the reporting organization's directors.

Question 6

Complete this question to reflect the legal status of the reporting organization under the laws of your province, or the statute governing the act of your incorporation.

Question 8

"Produced by this organization" means that the reporting organization took the financial risk involved in producing the master and that it has proprietary and copyright claim in the original sound recording. Canadian subsidiaries of foreign record companies which release records from their parent's catalogue do not produce that material and hence should indicate it as leased material.

Question 10

This also includes discs or tapes imported if your organization acted as an exclusive distributor on a territorial basis.

Question 12

Re-issues of older material should be counted as a new release *only* if the re-issue has a separate catalogue number from the original. Otherwise count only new releases. Place all 7″ formats regardless of speed under "7″ disc". Place all 12″ formats regardless of speed under "12″ disc". Do not count a tape format as a separate release *unless* the tape release was the only format of manufacture.

Question 13

A record consists of a number of selections or tunes. Some of these selections may qualify as Canadian content (as per CRTC regulations). Question 13 asks you to count the number of releases your organization manufactured by two criteria – origin of the master and whether or not a release has any Canadian content selections on it.

Question 14

Respondents are asked to use their own judgement when classifying music.

Question 16

An "act" is an artist or group name. Indicate in this question the number of acts, under contract to your organization, for whom you have released records.

Question 19
Net sales is net allowances for returns, if any. Question 19 refers to sales of discs and tapes only. Revenue from leasing agreements is reported in Question 20.

Question 20
Total revenue will consist of all leasing fees which you received including all portions of the fees which you may eventually have to pay out to artists, etc.

Question 21
This question asks for gross revenue (receipts) but net of sales taxes collected from customers, if any.

Question 22
"Recording costs" includes any recoupable advances, payments to musicians, vocalists, arrangers and copyists, studio costs, engineering costs (not laquer mastering), producer's salaries and expenses, and producer's royalties paid to producer during the financial year, if any. Only masters produced and *owned* by your organization are to be included here.

Question 23
"Lease fees and advances paid" includes AF of M Pension and Trust fees paid.

Question 24
Manufacturing costs include laquer mastering, pressing, duplicating, fabrication and designing of jackets and sleeves, liner notes and final packaging. Indicate costs for manufacturing outside of Canada separately.

Some Results of the Survey

Sales Revenue

Sixty-two of the seventy-four respondents reported that they had sales revenue from record and tapes manufactured in Canada amounting to $ 182.0 million[1] at the first point of delivery. The remaining twelve companies were master-tape production companies only, and did not release their own records themselves. This value represents the respondents' sales revenue from wholesale distributors and rack-jobbers, and in some cases, sales direct to retail outlets and the retail consumer.

During 1977, a typical popular music album with a suggested list price of $ 7.98 would have been sold by the reporting companies to wholesale distributors or rack-jobbers for approximately $ 4.20 plus or minus 5% depending on the volume of the order. These distributors would then in

---

[1] Net of Federal Sales Tax (12%) and allowances for returned items (10% is the industry standard). Sales are for the respondents' financial year ending between April 1, 1977 and March 31, 1978.

Table 1. *Revenue by Source, 1977*

Revenue[1] group	No. of companies reporting	Record and tape revenue[2]		Lease revenue		Revenue from related activities
		Domestic sales	Foreign sales	Domestic sales	Foreign sales	
I $ 0 – 99,999	47	662,136	13,364	214,371	×	2,253,742
II 100,000 – 999,999	12	3,413,251	294,747	878,233	×	2,600,231
III 1,000,000 – 9,999,999	8	55,527,828	×	×	×	19,878,911
IV 10,000,000 +	7	121,648,152	×	×	×	83,925,684
Total	74	181,251,367	779,511	2,372,688	1,380,768	108,658,568

[1] Revenue refers to sales of discs and tapes and revenue from the leasing or sales of master tapes. Revenue from *Related Activities* was not considered in grouping companies.
[2] From material manufactured in Canada.
× – confidential – included in total.

Table 2. *Revenue by Country of Control, 1977*

	Sales of discs and tapes and lease revenue	Related activities
Control:		
Canada ($N = 61$)	31,909,990	14,547,921
Foreign ($N = 13$)	153,874,449	94,110,647
Total ($N = 74$)	185,784,439	108,658,568

turn sell to other distributors or retail outlets in or outside of Canada. Revenue Canada data[2] show that approximately $ 2.9 million of discs were exported from Canada during 1977. The greater proportion of these exports were by distribution companies since this survey shows that only $ 779,511 (27%) of discs and tapes were exported by 13 of the reporting record companies themselves.

Sales by Origin of the Master-Tape and Country of Financial Control

Of the $ 182.0 million total sales revenue from discs and tapes manufactured in Canada, Canadian-controlled companies (49 of the 62 reporting record companies) accounted for $ 30.1 million or 16.5%. Of this $ 30.1 million, sales from masters either produced by the reporting companies or leased from other companies in Canada amounted to $ 7.2 million (24% of the $ 30.1 million). Sales from masters owned by companies outside of Canada amounted to $ 12.9 million (43% of the $ 30.1 million) while sales from unidentified masters made up the remainder of $ 10.0 million.

Sales by the 13 foreign controlled companies amounted to $ 151.9 million (83.5%) of the total $ 182.0 million sales revenue from discs and tapes manufactured in Canada. Of this $ 151.9 million, sales from masters owned by the respondents (the Canadian subsidiaries themselves) or from masters owned by other companies in Canada amounted to $ 30.1 million or about 20%. Sales from foreign-owned masters amounted to $ 107.5 million (71%). The remaining $ 14.3 million in sales could not be identified as to origin of the master.

Revenue from Lease Agreements: $ 3.8 Million

There were twelve small master-tape production companies, which along with the larger record companies, leased their master-tapes to other

___

[2] See Statistics Canada publication No. 65-004 "Exports by Commodities" December, 1977.

Table 3. *Record Releases by Revenue Group and Canadian Content, 1977*

Revenue[1] group:	No. of companies reporting releases	Canadian content		Non-Canadian content		Total	
		7" Discs	12" Discs	7" Discs	12" Discs	7" Discs	12" Discs
I $ 0 – 99,999	37	160	166	63	22	223	188
II 100,000 – 999,999	10	55	103	26	121	81	224
III 1,000,000 – 9,999,999	8	129	77	612	1,035	741	1,112
IV 10,000,000 +	7	182	153	1,083	1,472	1,265	1,625
Total	62[2]	526	499	1,784	2,650	2,310	3,149

[1] Revenue refers to sales of discs and tapes and revenue from the leasing or sales of master tapes.
[2] 12 additional companies reporting in this survey did not release records but were master-tape production companies only.

companies. The smaller companies, often consisting of no more than an artistic group, cannot handle the time and capital required to manufacture and distribute records, therefore they simply lease their masters to larger companies in exchange for a fee for every copy sold. Larger companies lease masters also, but not for the same reason. The larger companies lease masters to record companies in other trading areas (e.g. U.S.A.) or they lease to companies which specialize in "compilation" albums consisting of selections by different artists. The respondents involved in leasing masters earned $ 2.4 million in lease revenues from record manufacturers in Canada and $ 1.4 million from companies in other countries.

Revenue from Industry-Related Activities: $ 108.7 Million

Record companies are involved in many other activities besides selling their own records. The largest companies with their own manufacturing plants press the records of smaller companies, distribute other companies records, import records from other countries, produce master recordings for other companies, and own large chains of retail record outlets. This whole range of activities combined with earnings from artist management activities and earned royalties netted the recording industry $ 108.7 million or a value nearly equal to 60% of the revenue from disc and tape sales. The vertical integration of production, manufacturing, distribution, and retail sales is particularly important to a record company because it ensures an economy of scale and the availability to the public of all its product. Canadian-controlled companies earned only $ 14.5 million of the total $ 108.7 million or 13.4% indicating that the infrastructure of the Canadian recording industry is basically foreign controlled.

New Releases for 1977: 2310 Singles and 3149 Albums

Respondents reported that 526 (23%) of the total 2310 new singles had at least one selection qualifying as Canadian content (as per the CRTC regulations) and 1784 new singles (77%) with no Canadian content. Of the 3149 new albums, 499 (16%) were classified as having at least one Canadian content selection, and the remainder 2650 (84%) with none.

Forty-nine Canadian controlled companies manufactured 447 (19%) of the total 2310 new singles and 541 (17%) of the 3149 new albums released during 1977. Of this production by Canadian-controlled companies, 268 (60%) of the 447 singles and 294 (54%) of 541 new albums contained at least one selection qualifying as Canadian content.

The thirteen foreign-controlled companies manufactured 1863 (81%) of the 2310 new singles and 2608 (83%) of the 3149 new albums. Of these

Table 4. *Origin of Master Tape, Canadian Content, and Country of Financial Control*

	Canadian content		Non-Canadian content	
	7″ Singles	12″ Albums	7″ Singles	12″ Albums
Canadian Financial control:				
Produced by the reporting company	187	217	×	×
Leased from other companies in Canada	69	61	×	×
Leased from companies in other countries	12	16	×	207
Total	268	294	179	247
Foreign financial control:				
Produced by the reporting company	114	78	×	×
Leased from other companies in Canada	88	68	×	×
Leased from companies in other countries	56	59	1,599	2,387
Total	258	205	1,605	2,403
Total all Recordings	526	499	1,784	2,650

singles, 258 (14%) of the 1863 had at least one selection qualifying as Canadian content, while 205 (8%) of the 2608 albums did.

Over the last decade or two many Canadian artists have relocated in other countries to take advantage of the international record industry. When the Canadian subsidiaries of foreign record companies release these artists recordings in Canada, they often qualify as Canadian content. The number of releases qualifying as Canadian content from foreign-owned masters would be a rough indicator of the productivity of Canadian artists working in other countries. There were 56 singles and 59 albums qualifying as Canadian content that were released by foreign-controlled record companies in Canada from master tapes owned by companies in other countries. Canadian-controlled companies released 12 singles and 16 albums qualifying as Canadian-content from foreign owned masters.

Canadian content singles were made up of 45% Top 40, 25% Country and 20% Adult Popular Music, with other types of music and unidentified singles making up the remainder of 10%. The non-Canadian content singles were made up of 36% Top 40, 23% Adult Popular Music and 14% Country with other and unspecified singles making up 27%.

Canadian-content albums consisted of 30% Country, 22% Top 40, 19% Adult Popular Music, and other music and unspecified albums at 29%. Non-Canadian content albums consist of 26% Top 40, 16% Adult Popular Music and Classical at about 11%. Country and Jazz tied at about 9%. The remaining 29% was made up of other music and unspecified albums. In the albums as well as the singles, Country music was more common in the Canadian-content records than in records with no Canadian content.

Language of Releases

Of the 526 Canadian content singles released during 1977, 105 or 20% were French language, 370 or 70% were English language while the remaining 51 (10%) were made up of other languages, instrumental or unidentified recordings (hereinafter simply called "other").

Table 5. *Language of Recording, Canadian Content, and Country of Financial Control*

	Canadian content		Non-Canadian content	
	7″ Singles	12″ Albums	7″ Singles	12″ Albums
Canadian financial control:				
English lyrics	203	146	156	199
French lyrics	58	75	0	0
Other, including unspecified recordings and instrumental music	7	73	23	48
Total	268	294	179	247
Foreign financial control:				
English lyrics	167	118	1,161	1,450
French lyrics	47	51	144	116
Other, including unspecified recordings and instrumental music	44	36	300	837
Total	258	205	1,605	2,403
Total all recordings	526	499	1,784	2,650

The 499 Canadian-content albums consisted of 126 (25%) French language recordings, 264 (53%) English language, with the remaining 109 (23%) made up of "other".

Insofar as non-Canadian content records are concerned, only 144 (8%) of the 1784 singles were French language recordings, while 116 (4%) of the 2650 albums had French lyrics. All of the French language non-Canadian content recordings were released by foreign controlled companies.

Conclusion

The results of the recording survey have been well received. One of the associations representing the industry has used the data to state its case for modifications to the existing taxation structure of the record industry. Both of the associations have disseminated copies of the results to their members and have held meetings to discuss the results among themselves. At least one federal government department has used the results in an internal document that analyzes the positive and negative implications of proposed changes to the laws of copyright as this affects the sound recording industry.

We feel that the recording survey is adequate to measure production, content, and revenues but the survey could be modified to include a balance sheet and a profit and loss statement. These items would allow for a financial analysis of the industry. Such information would be of use to policy-makers as well as to the industry itself.

General Bibliography

Shemel, Sidney, Krasilovsky, M. William, *This Business of Music* – Revised and Enlarged Copyright Act Edition. Billboard Publications Inc., New York 1977.

Shemel, Sidney, Krasilovsky, M. William, *More About This Business of Music*. Billboard Publications Inc., New York 1974.

EMI Limited, *World Record Markets*. EMI Limited, 20 Manchester Square, London W1A 1ES.

Klopchic, P., *Sector Analysis – the Record Industry in Ontario*. Ministry of Industry and Tourism (Ontario) 1976.

Krister Malm

Phonograms and Cultural Policy in Sweden

1. Bounds, Definitions, Basic Information

Terminology

In this report a *phonogram* or *record* is defined as a vehicle of recorded sound and, when applicable, its packaging including text and illustrations. The *field of phonograms* or *sound recordings* is defined so as to include all the resources and processes necessary for producing, distributing, and listening to sound recordings.

This report is concerned mainly with those parts of the sound recording field at present considered most problematical from the point of view of cultural politics. The actual manufacturing of various types of vehicles of recorded sound and of various kinds of technical equipment is touched upon only briefly.

Some of the terms used in the following material are defined below:

Record companies are organizations responsible for producing and issuing sound recordings.

Recording units are organizations that provide studio facilities and technical equipment: they make sound recordings but are not involved in issuing them.

Pressing and copying companies mass-reproduce sound recordings.

Distribution companies are responsible for wholesaling.

A record label is the trademark shown on the label or cover of a sound recording. One record company may produce sound recordings on several different record labels.

An issue is a number of sound recordings with the same content.

An incidental producer is a person or a group of persons responsible for producing and issuing occasional sound recordings, normally a maximum of one recording a year. (A record company must issue at least two sound recordings a year in order to qualify for membership in a trade association.)

A repertoire category consists of a certain kind of music (or other material) published in the form of a sound recording. For purposes of comparison, sound recordings have been divided into seven categories used in all studies conducted in connection with this report. These categories are:

Art music, Western art music, or, as it has been called in questionnaires, "classical and modern serious music". This category comprises both old and new art music within the European tradition, e.g. orchestral music, chamber music, choir music, and opera.

Folk music and singing comprises both Swedish and foreign traditional folk music and singing. (The products of the folk music revival are also included in this category.)

Religious songs, including gospel music.

Pop music includes rock and pop music of the North American and English types plus Swedish pop music inspired by these.

Dance music and other popular music includes hit songs, music from the native Swedish showbands, etc.

Recordings for children (childrens' records) are those that are intended to appeal especially to children — e.g. fairy tales, musical fairy tales, songs for children, etc.

Other sound recordings include everything not included in one of the above categories, particularly the spoken-word record.

This type of categorization — for practical and methodological reasons — must be very sketchy. The above classification is based on Swedish research in the sociology of music.

The most important stages in the development of a sound recording, from conception to turntable, are:

1) production, including planning, recording, editing, and mass production;

2) distribution, consisting of marketing, wholesale and retail trade;

3) reception (via purchase, loan, or mass media) and use.

The description of the sound recording field in this report is based upon the above classification.

"Commercial" and "Noncommercial"

The terms "commercial" and "noncommercial" have been used frequently in writings on records in Sweden. These terms are normally used to describe both a record company's mode of operation and the nature of particular records, e.g. "a commercial sound".

One of the aims of government policy on culture in Sweden is to counteract the negative effects of commercialism. Profitability shall not be allowed to control cultural activities. This means that the appropriate authorities must play an active role whenever the activities of individuals in the cultural field are unable to guarantee a sufficiently diversified production, or in some other way fail to meet official demands.

It is difficult to find a cogent definition of the word "commercialism". The term has been used in many ways. A relevant description was offered in 1974 by the then minister of education in the government bill on "State Cultural Policy":

The pursuit of profits leads to efforts, via advertising and other means of manipulation, to influence consumption without regard for the importance of various needs. There are many examples of unbridled commercialism in the area of culture, often consisting of speculation in trivialities. Large groups of people, in particular the young, are subjected to the sole influence of cultural products that are shabby and inferior, e.g. products speculating in violence.˙ In extensive cultural areas the private cultural industry has a measure of power that gives it a dominant role in shaping attitudes: as an exploiter of these attitudes, it is interested in supplying products that are acceptable to as many people as possible. This leads to a cultural content which neither provokes nor furthers critical attitutes and which demands passivity on the part of the consumer.

Another consequence of commercial production or distribution is that even products of a serious nature have difficulty meeting the demands made by society: activities are concentrated into areas yielding the highest profit, thus discouraging variety and innovation. Nor can professional artists be guaranteed a dependable and reasonable living by private culture industry: they are often forced to regulate their artistic activities purely in the interests of profit.

In 1975 a special trade association, the Association of Noncommercial Nordic Phonogram Producers (NIFF), was founded by a number of record companies who regard themselves as noncommercial. These companies more or less subscribe to what is stated about commercialism in "State Cultural Policy".

In paragraphs two and three of NIFF's statutes the association states its criteria for deciding whether or not a record company is noncommercial:

2. Through its cultural policy, particularly in the field of music, the association shall support the development of progressive culture and combat the commercialization of culture.

3. Membership of the association may be granted to any juridical person who

a) subscribes to the aims of the association,

b) has produced at least two sound recordings and regularly produces at least two sound recordings a year,

c) works in such a way that the enterprise can be judged to be governed not by speculation in profits but by progressive cultural aims,

d) has a democratic decision-making structure with a high degree of influence on the part of the artists or a structure constituting part of a progressively aligned organization,

e) is not owned by individuals.

Outside NIFF as well, there are a number of record companies for whom profit plays a subordinate role in determining the range of activities.

In a list of technical terms in "Ljudspåren förskräcker" (p. 224) Per-Anders Hellqvist writes regarding the term "commercialism":

The sense of this word can be factual, emotional, or moralizing according to the context in which it appears. In this book I mean by "commercial" a product or issue the main purpose of which is to generate profits at the stages of production and distribution (e.g. to shareholders). A record may well be "noncommercial" even if the musicians involved are paid for their labours—it is the pursuit of compensation out of proportion to the amount of work performed that qualifies a product for the label "commercial".

The limits, apparently, are somewhat vague. If the company responsible for a product consists of a musicians' collective, with no outside (share) owners, and the company generally works without profit motives but with the intention of returning all net income to the musicians, then it is doubtful whether the enterprise can be called "noncommercial". But if the "profits" are all ploughed back in the form of a subsidy to a product incurring losses for the same enterprise, then it is obviously noncommercial.

Several researchers at the Institute of Musicology at the University of Gothenburg have studied commercialism in the music field. Stig-Magnus

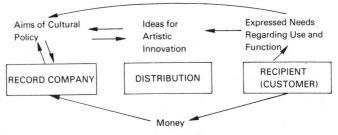

Fig. 1. Model of communication for the field of sound recordings

Thorsén, in an article entitled "What Is Meant by Commercial Music?" (Tonfallet no. 7, 1976), has presented a model devised by the Gothenburg researchers. This model is related to the musical chain-of-communication presented by Ingmar Bengtsson in the book Musikvetenskap (1973). Thorsén's model is easily applicable to the field of sound recordings, as in Fig. 1.

This flowchart is combined with the following chart dealing with certain characteristics typical of commercial and noncommercial recording enterprises.

Characteristics of Commercial Recording Enterprises

Noncommercial Recording Enterprises

The record company is a firm in which decisions are made by shareholders and management. Writers and artists are aligned in a strict hierarchy. Various people have highly specialized tasks in the production machinery. Production planning is governed mainly by the lust for profits. Profits go to shareholders.

The aim of marketing is to create a demand by manipulating recipients. Mass distribution of each individual product to as many people as possible.

Representatives for the recipients and collectives of authors and/or performers make the decision (sometimes singly). Production-planning is governed mainly by expressed needs and artistic innovation. Profits, if any, are used to promote new products or for other nonprofit purposes.

Marketing is focused on consumer information. There is an effort to distribute records to those groups of recipients who need them.

In brief, one might say that, in any given record company, the more activity that occurs in the lower path of circulation on the flowchart, the more commercial the company is. Both paths of circulation are present in the activities of most record companies in Sweden. Most of these companies could, then, be placed on a scale ranging from commercial to noncommercial depending on the degree to which their activities are governed by the needs of the customer, artistic ideas, aims of cultural policy, and the desire for profits. No exact method exists for measuring the level of commercialism in the sound recording field. However, it is possible to make rough judgements, and it is easier to judge whether a single product is commercial or noncommercial than to evaluate the whole of a company's production.

Often certain parts of a company's production are generally commercial while other parts are noncommercial. In spite of the fact that the terms "commercial" and "noncommercial" do not possess an exact meaning, they are well-established in the sound recording field and in that line of business have a sufficiently clear meaning to be of use (according to the above definitions) to indicate roughly the direction and certain characteristics of activities.

Copyright

Terms of copyright in the sound recording field in Sweden are governed by the Swedish copyright law and by two international conventions – the Rome Convention of 1961 and the Convention for the Protection of Producers of Phonograms against Unauthorized Duplication of their Phonograms of 1971 – both of which have been ratified by Sweden. A more detailed description of the main features of the copyright situation will be found in the conventions themselves.

Guiding Principles in the Marketing of Gramophone Records and Cassettes

An agreement concerning the packaging of gramophone records and cassettes, made between the Consumer Ombudsman and, among others, the Swedish group of IFPI, has been in effect since 1976. The terms of this agreement are roughly as follows:

Faulty copies of sealed records retailed in Sweden should be exchangeable even when the seal has been broken.

According to an international agreement record sleeves should be marked with the symbol ℗ ("published") and the year.

This information concerning the *year of publication* should always be on the sleeve, if the *year of recording* should fail to coincide with the year of publication – e.g. in cases of reissue of old recordings – then the year of recording should also be stated. If a record consists of recordings from different years, then the year of recording for each item should be stated by the side of the item.

Cover Recordings, i.e. copies that a lesser-known orchestra makes of hits made by well-known artists, should in accordance with the agreement bear labels stating "Not the original artists" or "Not the original version".

Regarding *participants*, it shall be stated if certain members of a well-known orchestra have been replaced by studio musicians during recording. In this case the sleeve should bear the text "Studio musicians have participated in this recording".

Some double albums have been sold in *sealed plastic covers* which have been impossible to open without breaking the seal, in spite of the fact that all important information about the record has been on the inside spread.

The Swedish record companies agreed to refrain from selling such double albums.

Recordings are normally made in stereo these days. Thus, *monorecordings* should clearly be labeled as such.

The above agreement concerning year of publication, participants, sealed sleeves, and mono recordings is basically applicable to records produced in Sweden. Representatives of the trade have in addition expressed an intention to encourage their foreign partners to abide by these guiding principles.

2. Research in Sound Recordings

Considering the fact that sound recordings have been in existence for over one hundred years and have been an important mass medium since the 1920s, surprisingly little research has been done on them. Few attempts have been made to summarize what is known about the general importance of sound recordings in society as a whole and the world of music in particular. Most of the research carried out in the sound recording field has dealt with methods of recording playback and mass production. Some studies have been made of the organization and way of working of the international record industry. These studies examine, among other things, attitudes governing the operations of the large multinational record companies as well as the structure of these companies, and their marketing methods plus the influence exerted by the record industry upon change and growth in various categories of music.

Specialized market research studies are performed by the record companies. This research is concerned with the salient characteristics of various target groups. Results of the research are used in marketing drives and are kept confidential by the companies. A few studies have been made apart from company research, on the use of sound recordings and their function for the recipient.

Two major studies on the situation in the sound recording field in Sweden have been carried out in conjunction with the work of the sound recordings group of the National Council for Cultural Affairs.

The National Price and Cartel Board (SPK) has studied the development of prices and the degree of competition in the sound recording field in Sweden during the 1970s. The results are presented in a report dealing with the structure of the record industry and retail trade in Sweden, the range and direction of production and sales, the costs of production of various types of sound recording, service to customers, pricetrends profitability, etc.

The distribution of various types of sound systems and consumer behavior of record buyers have been the subject of a joint study by the secretariat of the sound recording group and the Audience and Program Research Department of the Swedish Broadcasting Company (SR/PUB).

Most of the information related in this report concerning the state of the sound recording field has been gleaned from these two studies.

Research Assignments for the Future

A great many areas are yet to be researched in the field of sound recordings. Existing information today either covers only certain parts of this field (inadequately) or else constitutes company secrets. This is because most of the research carried out to date has been governed by short-term needs in musical institutions or the record industry. Very little research has been designed to examine the field of sound recordings in terms of the aims of cultural policy and the deeper needs of various groups of recipients. More systematic free research in the sound recording field is of the utmost importance, among other reasons in order to facilitate effective public action.

Future research in the sound recording field ought to be based on a comprehensive view of this field as a social, cultural, and economic system of the type shown in the sketch below (Fig. 2).

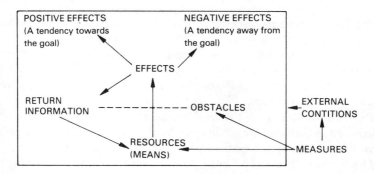

Fig. 2. Model for the organization of research in the sound recording field

For purposes of formulating cultural policies, but also for other reasons, this system could be studied in order to shed light on the relationship between methods and aims in the sound recording field. Here is assumed that there is a conscious will to achieve certain goals by means of those measures taken by public as well as private interests. The supposed purpose of public measures is to approach the established goals of cultural policies. It should be possible to organize research based on the above according to this model:

The system inside the frame is the sound recording field. Within this field subsystems can be defined, e.g. an international system, domestic (Swedish) system, a commercial system, a noncommercial system, etc.

The field as a whole is affected by certain external conditions such as laws prevailing ideologies, trade policies, raw material resources, infrastructure, information technology, etc.

In the sound recording field there are certain controls and resources in the form of technique, finance, decision-making routines, systems of administration, etc. upon which the present forms of production and distribution are based. The effects these resources have on the community also depend upon which obstacles (filters or barriers) exist in the field. These obstacles may be structural – e.g., trade structure, organizational structure, demographic factors, income conditions, etc. – or they may take the form of human behaviour on a psychological or social level, such as various personal needs, record-listening habits and such.

The combination of controls, resources, and obstacles leads to effects that can be defined as positive (those that lead to the adopted goals) and negative (those that do not).

A detailed study of the use of available controls and resources requires a continuous feedback of information from the effect area to the control/resources area, for example, statistics such as sales returns for various record products, changes in program policy on the part of radio and TV, etc.

The whole system can be affected by actions taken by a number of parties. These measures may consist of changes in external conditions and/or changes regarding controls, resources, and obstacles. With the help of the above model (Fig. 2) it is possible to identify a number of important research assignments.

Viewed as a whole research in the sound recording field is an international question to be dealt with by researchers from a number of countries. But from the narrower point-of-view of Swedish cultural policies, certain research assignments ought to be given priority: those having a direct bearing upon actions taken by Swedish government bodies in the field of sound recordings. Such assignments include:

— a survey of the effects of measures taken by government bodies within the sound recording field;

— a survey of what kind of continuous information, such as statistics concerning the sound recording field is needed to facilitate effective action on the part of government bodies;
— and a survey to define which parts of the controls — resources — obstacles complex can be affected by Swedish cultural policies and which parts are determined by external conditions (international or internal).

3. The Economics of the Sound Recording Field

The United States are by far the largest record market in the world (Table 1): sales of records in 1976 totalled $ 2.7 billion. Japan, the next

Table 1. *The Value of Records Sold in 1976 in Various Countries* (*Retail Prices*)

Country	Sales value in U.S. $ M (retail prices)	Per capita sales values (U.S. $)
U.S.	2,737	13
Japan	738	6
Fed. Rep. of Germany	700	12
France	538	11
Great Britain	430	8
Canada	295	13
Australia	160	12
Brazil	156	1
Sweden	147	18
Italy	143	3
The Netherlands	126	9
Mexico	114	2
Spain	80	2
Belgium	73	7
Switzerland	60	9
Argentina	54	2
Austria	53	7
Denmark	51	10
Norway	46	11
South Africa	42	2
Finland	35	7

Source: Billboard International Buyer's Guide 1977/78, section 2, 1977-09-17 (columns 1 and 2; column 3 = own calculations)

largest market, has but one-fourth of U.S. sales. Sweden is in the ninth place in the West (5% of U.S. sales). Sweden, however, has by far the highest per capita record sales, with an average in 1976 of $ 18 per person.

The U.S. and Canada come next with $ 13 per person. The Swedish market is relatively important from an international point of view, but hardly large enough for the likes and dislikes of Swedish record-buyers to play any appreciable part in decisions made by multinational record companies as to the contents of their products.

Table 2. *Sales of Records and Nonrecorded Cassettes 1965 – 1977. Millions of Copies*

Year	Number		
	Records total (millions of copies)	Of which music cassettes (millions of copies)	Unrecorded cassettes (millions of copies)
1965	4		
6	5		0.1
7	6		0.1
8	8		0.2
9	9		0.3
1970	9		0.6
1	11		1.0
2	11	0.5	1.7
3	13	0.9	3.0
4	14	1.4	6.5
5	17	2.8	8.5
6	20	3.2	9.5
7	21	4.0	11.0

Sources: The Marketing Department of Svenska Philips and The Swedish Price and Cartel Board.

In terms of economic indices (Tables 2 and 3) the record industry has shown the highest expansion rate of all Swedish mass media during the 1970s – an increase of 106 percent during 1970 – 76, as compared with 38 percent for the daily press and 23 percent for TV and radio. This increase reflects a great deal of interest in records. The prices of records and record hardware have more or less remained unchanged throughout the 1970s.

Table 3. *Expenditure on Mass Media Consumption in Sweden in the Years of 1970 and 1976. Total Costs, Costs Per Medium and Type of Costs Per Medium Plus the Share of Each Medium in the Mass Media Economy*

Type of consumption and type of costs	Million of Swedish crowns p.a		Change 1970 – 76	Percentage share of mass media economy	
	1970	1976	%	1970	1976
Dailies	2,525	3,700	+ 47	33	34
Subscriptions and single copies	1,056	1,500			
Advertisements	1,464	2,030			
State aid	5	170			
Periodicals	1,405	1,729	+ 23	18	16
Subscriptions and single copies	882	1,130			
Advertisements	392	435			
Organizational grants	131	160			
Dailies and periodicals	3,930	5,429	+ 38	51	50
Radio	708	808	+ 14	9	7
Licence fees and taxes	278	291			
Sets, aerials	294	410			
Repairs, energy	136	107			
TV	1,860	2,341	+ 26	24	22
Licence fees and taxes	568	586			
Sets, aerials	1,146	1,570			
Repairs, energy, hire of sets	146	185			
Radio and TV	2,568	3,149	+ 23	33	29
Gramophone	738	1,340	+ 86	9	12.5
Sets	478	800			
Records	250	525			
Repairs	(10)	(15)			
Cassette recorders	195	585	+ 200	3	5.5
Sets	186	355			
Cassettes	(9)	220			
Repairs	–	10			
Gramophon and cassettes	933	1,925	+ 106	12	18

Table 3 (continued)

Type of consumption and type of costs	Million of Swedish crowns p.a		Change 1970 – 76	Percentage share of mass media economy	
	1970	1976	%	1970	1976
Film	294	313	+ 6	4	3
Cinema tickets	283	296			
Advertizing incomes	6	12			
State aid	–	5			
Film	294	313	+ 6	4	3
Total	7,725	10,820	+ 36		

Millions of Swedish crowns at the price index obtaining in 1976. Source: SR/PUB, Ivre

Costs of Record Production in Sweden

The costs of record production comprise fixed costs and variable costs.

Fixed costs comprise the costs of recording and matrix – engraving plus certain overhead costs such as the wages of permanent employees and rental of premises. Recording costs include singers/musicians, rental of studio, employment of technicians, assistants, producers and the like.

Variable costs comprise partly costs of record and sleeve massproduction, partly royalties to artists and composers/authors.

The costs of marketing, sales and distribution are partly fixed costs (product launching) and partly variable costs (costs of freight, warehousing, etc.).

A breakdown of the total costs of Swedish record production 1975 – 77 is found in Table 4.

The costs of record production in Sweden vary greatly according to the nature of the product.

In 1976, the average cost of production (studio- or live-recording) for small groups was Sw.Cr. 110,000. Average sales, 1974 – 77, totalled 9,500 copies. A record company can generally count on covering costs when about 6,500 copies of a record are sold.

Generally then, the production of records in Sweden is a relatively profitable undertaking. But the production of records with certain types of music is clearly unprofitable. Average sales in the areas of Western art

Table 4. *Distribution of Costs of All Swedish Record
Production During the Period 1975 – 1977*

Type of costs	% of total costs	
Fixed costs		
Costs of recording (including wages)	17	
Engraving + matrix	2	
Marketing	8	
Administration and other fixed costs	16	
Partial total		43
Variable costs		
Pressing, copying, sleeves	31	
Royalties to participants	10	
Royalties to copyright owners	11	
Distribution	5	
Partial total		57
Total		100

Background: Data from surveys conducted by the Swedish
Price and Cartel Board.

music, folk music and jazz totalled but 3,000 copies: the production of a
record in these areas implied an average loss of around Sw.Cr. 20,000.
Sw.Cr. 100 = approx. U.S. $ 23:50.

4. The Production of Records

The productions of records involves all the stages up to the mass
production of a record. These different stages may exist within a single
company, but are normally split up between a number of companies.
These companies may belong to one and the same concern or they may
have different owners. Record companies are responsible for putting the
finishing touches to a record and issuing it.

The production of records in the West is dominated by a handfull of
multinational concerns: the five largest sell 60 percent of all records in the
West. These are: CBS (U.S.), EMI (Great Britain), Polygram (West
Germany – Holland), Warner Communications (U.S.), and RCA (U.S.).
The production of records is only one of the activities of these
concerns – they are also involved in other mass media, electronics, etc.

Each concern releases records on a number of labels. All the concerns
own subsidiaries outside their home countries. CBS, EMI, and Polygram
have Swedish subsidiaries that in turn own other companies in Sweden. In

1977 these three concerns were responsible for 56 percent of record sales in Sweden.

The concentration of the international record industry has been rapid during the 1970s. Smaller companies have been bought up by the large concerns, thus granting the large multinational record concerns more and more influence upon the contents of record products around the world. To a great extent they decide which records are to be offered to record buyers in various countries. They can, via their multinational marketing organizations, create a world wide demand for certain records.

Horizontal and Vertical Integration

Record companies, like many other companies, strive to gather or integrate as many functions as possible into one company in order to decrease costs and increase profits. Up to the beginning of the 1970s, most stages in record production were spread over many companies. During the 1970s a fairly rapid integration has taken place. This integration can.be divided into two kinds: horizontal integration, which involves mergers between similar activity groups such as those involved in the composition and arranging of music, managerial functions, music publishing, TV, radio, and film production; and vertical integration, which involves the merging of distinct stages in the path of a record from idea to record buyer such as production, marketing, distribution, and retailing. These processes of integration take place at both international and national levels.

One method of horizontal integration involves the purchase of music publishing houses by record companies. Sheet music is not issued primarily for sale but to allow record companies to recoup money which they have paid to copyright organizations for publishing rights. Another type of horizontal integration is to bind an artist to a record company via an "exclusive contract" and also handle PR and management for these artists. Composers, arrangers, graphic arts designers, etc. are also "bought" by record companies.

Vertical integration implies that a record company establishes or buys recording studios, record pressing and cassette copying plants, printing works, distribution companies, and retail companies.

Record Companies and Their Trade Associations in Sweden

Apart from the Swedish subsidiaries of CBS, EMI, and Polygram, there are around sixty record companies in Sweden. Most of these companies are relatively small in terms of turnover, but play an important role in Swedish record production from the point of view of cultural policies. Most of the small companies specialize in one particular repertoire category while the larger Swedish-owned companies usually issue records in several repertoire categories with pop music and dance music clearly in the lead.

There are two trade associations for record companies in Sweden. Eleven of the larger firms, including the subsidiaries of the multinational concerns, comprise the Swedish group of the International Federation of Producers of Phonograms and Videograms (IFPI). The Association of Noncommercial Nordic Phonogram Producers (NIFF) has nineteen members, all of them small Swedish-owned companies. Most record companies in Sweden do not belong to either of these two associations. These nonaffiliated companies are usually very small.

Apart from the products of the record companies, a number of records are issued each year in Sweden by various groups and individuals. STIM (the Swedish International Copyright Bureau) produces a number of records annually as part of the bureau's attempts to spread knowledge of the works of Swedish composers.

The Extent and Content of Swedish Record Production

Swedish record production has, according to the survey made by SPK, totalled around 800 – 900 issues a year. This figure consists mainly of issues of new Swedish recordings. Only around 5 percent of the products are re-issues of material previously available in the form of a record.

Around 40 percent, or 350 records annually contain dance music and hit music. Western art music, pop music, and religious songs total around 100 records each. The remaining 150 records consist of children's records (approx. 40), jazz (approx. 35), folk music (approx. 25), and others (approx. 50).

The multinational companies and the larger domestic companies were responsible for the publication of around 55 percent of the records containing Western art music and around 65 percent of the records with pop music and dance music.

Facilities for the recording and massproduction of records are relatively plentiful in Sweden today. However, there is a risk that EMI, via its pressing plant in Åmål, might assume a monopolistic position in the future; such a development can hardly be regarded as desirable.

5. Import to Sweden

Records are mainly imported by Swedish distribution companies that have been appointed as Swedish agents by foreign record companies. The Swedish agent does not normally stock copies of all records issued by foreign companies. Copies of about 3,800 records are imported to Sweden each year. About 60 percent of the titles in the catalogues of Swedish distributors are imported. Most imported records come from the U.S. and Great Britain, and records from these countries dominate the Swedish market thanks to the international marketing campaigns launched by the big concerns. The Federal Republic of Germany plays a major role in the market for Western art music. In spite of the fact that there is considerable record production in all the European countries — and also in the Third World — only a very small share of the import of records to Sweden comes from countries other than the three named above.

It is important to end this one-sided dependency upon the U.S. and Great Britain and replace it with channels for the import of records from many different countries.

6. Marketing, Sales, Distribution

Marketing consists of a number of different measures taken to ensure that the public is conscious of the availability of a certain record. Marketing methods used for each particular record depend to a great extent upon the nature of the contents of the record. There are generally two basic attitudes toward records, which also affect their marketing:

1. A record is regarded mainly as commodity to be marketed in the same way as other commodities. The recipients are regarded as buyers/consumers.

2. A record is regarded mainly as a part of cultural life, which implies methods of marketing emphasizing the cultural function and content of the various products. The recipients are regarded as participants in cultural life.

The first way of viewing records is at present the most common in the record trade, dominating as it does the marketing methods of the commercial companies. The second approach is to be found in lesser sectors of the large companies' operations and is common among small noncommercial record companies.

A view of the records as a mere commodity affects the whole process of production, wherein marketing and market research are seen as an integrated part of the planning of the contents and design of a product.

Marketing is effected via a number of established channels, including radio, TV, the press, and various types of advertizing material for the retail trade. Radio and TV are most important: their marketing role has been developed along the lines of the situation in the U.S. where paid advertizing for records on radio and TV play major role as do charts. Many Swedish TV- and radio programs are based on their counterparts in the U.S. and Great Britain.

Programs based on charts are presented by the Swedish Broadcasting Corporation, a fact which has drawn a lot of criticism, not least from

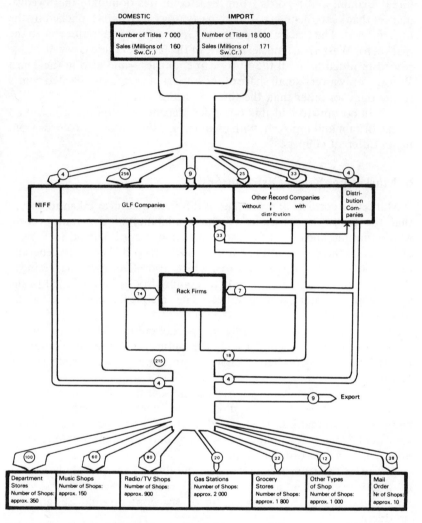

Fig. 3. How the sales of records was divided between different types of distributors in Sweden 1976. Millions of Swedish crowns at wholesale prices. Source: The Swedish Price and Cartel Board

representatives of the noncommercial record companies. Most transmission time on Swedish radio is devoted to music from records. The program policy of the Swedish Broadcasting Corporation with regard to records has a decisive effect on which records are produced and how many of them are sold in Sweden.

The wholesale record trade in Sweden consists partially of distribution companies directly connected either to one record company or to a group of record companies, and partially of independent distribution companies.

The independent group consists of both normal distribution companies and of rack firms. Figure 3 shows how total sales of records may be divided into various channels.

The four largest distribution companies in Sweden belong to the Association of Gramophone Suppliers (GLF). These four companies are: EMI Svenska AB (EMI Swedish Ltd); Grammofon AB Electra; CBS Records AB; Grammofonbolagens distributionscentral (GDC) i.e. (roughly) "the record companies' distribution centre". EMI, CBS, and Electra are each part of their respective record companies while GDC is owned by five record companies.

The companies affiliated to GLF have dominated sales of records in Sweden during the 1970s. Their share of total sales in 1976 was 87 percent. GLFs role is more or less oligopolistic: its size allows it to dictate norms and limits for all Swedish sales and distribution of records.

Around forty — mostly small — record companies distribute their records through channels other than GLF. Some of these companies attend to their own distribution, others distribute their records via independent distribution companies.

The small distribution companies — with only a few exceptions — have had difficulties in asserting themselves, which is unfortunate as the records they distribute are often of importance from the point of view of cultural policy.

The rack firms normally buy their records from other distributors. Then they come to an agreement with chain stores or shop owners allowing them to place a rack of records on the premises. The rack firm decides what is to be sold and ensures that the rack is kept well-stocked. The shopowner gets a cut of the proceeds.

There are at present three large rack firms in Sweden. The largest is Grammo Rack Service AB which is owned collectively by the GLF companies. A rapid increase in the rack firms' share of record sales has occurred since 1974: in 1976 they were responsible for 27% of all sales.

Retail sales of records take place mainly via department stores, music shops, radio shops, and racks in various types of shop such as food shops, gas stations and kiosks.

In 1976 there were around 6,500 sales outlets. Only around 750 of these had special record departments; around 5,750 sold via racks. In addition there are 9 mail order firms (see Table 5).

Table 5. *Retail Sales of Records in 1976 (Retail Prices, Exclusive of VAT, in Millions of Swedish Crowns)*

Type of shop	Number of shops		Sales MSw. crowns Excl. VAT	Procentual share	
	Total	Rack shops		Shops	Sales
Department stores/supermarkets	350	190	138	5	29
Music shops	150	10	79	2	16
Radio/TV shops	900	590	108	14	23
Other shops	5,100	4,960	95	79	20
All shops	6,500	5,750	420	100	88
Mail order companies	9	–	58	0	12
Total	6,509	5,750	478	100	100

Source: Swedish Price and Cartel Board

The main characteristic of record retailing is that there are many sales outlets with relatively low sales volumes. Almost every other point of sale had a volume below Sw.Cr. 20,000 in 1976.

The 1970s have seen a change from sales via music and radio shops with knowledgeable assistants to (1) rack sales via small sales outlets lacking knowledgeable assistants and (2) a concentration toward a few large stores in the cities. Shops with a special record department are lacking in 80 percent of urban areas with a population under 10,000.

Mail order sales of records in 1976 were mainly the province of nine firms. The combined sales of these firms were around 12 percent of total sales. The largest mail order firm, Prestige AB, is part of the Polygram concern.

Records sales have increased greatly since 1970: from 9 million records in 1970 to around 21 million records in 1977 (see Table 2, page 53, and Fig. 4). This great increase is partially related to the introduction of cassettes to the market. Increases in sales have died down in recent years, and preliminary figures for 1978 point to a decrease in the number of records sold. The Swedish products' share in total sales has increased from about a third in 1971 to almost a half in 1977. The stagnation in total sales, however, has brought about a decline in the share of sales enjoyed by Swedish products. In the lists of the record distributors in 1977 there were 18,500 different records of which 4,500 were of Swedish origin. 54 percent of these records, and 78 percent of sales volume, consisted of pop and dance music. Table 6 shows in greater detail the apportionment of publishing and sales into various repertoire categories.

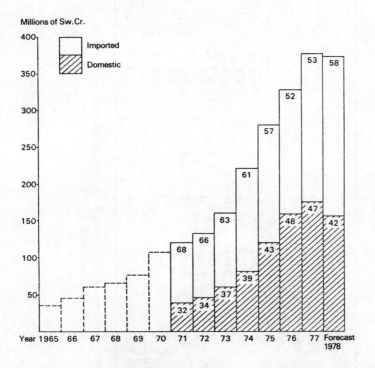

Fig. 4. Sales of records, 1965 – 1978. Wholesale prices in millions of Swedish crowns. Source: Swedish Price and Cartel Board

The concentration of sales upon relatively few records is extremely pronounced. From July 1, 1976, to July 1, 1977, just 30 records – i.e. 0.15 percent of the total number of records for sale – were responsible for almost 20 percent of sales. This reflects both the concentration of marketing resources on the part of the commercial companies to only a few records and the very limited range reaching the majority of customers via rack sales. The average range presented by various types of point of sale can be seen in Table 7.

In 1977 the vast majority of rack sales outlets had a range of around 200 records, consisting almost exclusively of pop and dance music. There is also a strong concentration upon pop and dance music in the case of other types of sales outlets. In 1977 there were only 300 sales outlets with a range

Table 6. *Number of Titles Plus the Distribution of Sales Between Swedish and Imported Records and Various Repertoire Categories in 1977*

Repertoire category	Domestic — Titles number	%	Number of records sold %	Import — Titles number	%	Number of records sold %	Total — Titles number	%	Number of records sold %
Art music	580	8	5	4,890	27	8	5,470	22	6
Folk music	370	5	3	720	4	0	1,090	4	2
Jazz	520	7	1	2,650	15	4	3,170	13	1
Religious songs	460	7	4	150	1	1	610	2	3
Pop music	900	13	22	6,390	35	66	7,290	29	36
Dance music	3,320	47	54	3,010	17	20	6,240	25	42
Children's records	390	6	7	0	0	0	390	2	5
Others	500	7	4	390	2	1	890	3	3
Total	6,950	100	100	18,200	100	100	25,150	100	100

Recordings issued both as records and as cassettes are counted as two titles. Thus, the number of titles in this table is not the same as the number of records issued, which without this double counting, totals 18,500.

Table 7. *Average Number of Titles in 1977 at Various Types of Sales Outlets with Sales in Various Repertoire Categories*

Type of sales outlet	Repertoire category								
	Total number of titles	Art music	Folk music	Jazz	Religious songs	Pop Music	Dance music	Children's music	Others
Shops with a special record department:									
Department stores/supermarkets	2,090	202	106	105	83	825	518	126	125
Music shops	4,362	781	189	289	158	1,971	711	136	127
Radio/TV shops	2,885	209	109	139	77	1,642	539	105	65
Other shops	2,089	182	60	72	68	1,208	331	78	90
All such shops	2,848	305	116	148	93	1,446	533	112	95
Rack shops:									
Department stores/supermarkets	792	47	30	51	33	314	245	46	26
Radio/TV shops	438	18	17	14	22	175	156	21	15
Other shops	133	3	7	8	6	52	42	11	4
All such shops	244	13	11	14	12	91	78	16	9
Total	786	72	33	42	29	374	173	36	27

Source: Swedish Price and Cartel Board.

of more than 100 records in each of the following repertoire categories: Western art music, folk music, jazz, religious songs, pop, dance music, and other popular music and childrens' records.

Service to customers is, for the most part, very poor. It is almost impossible to order records no longer in stock at the retail level except in the case of a few specialty shops with knowledgeable assistants. This is partly because no catalogue exists listing all records available in Sweden: this information is scattered throughout a number of small catalogues and adverting sheets from each record company.

The main reason for the restructuring of the retail trade and the poor service to customers is the policy regarding prices and conditions of supply practiced by the GLF group.

At the distributor level, there is a very firmly fixed wholesale price which, in practice, is set by the GLF group: this price can be altered via discounts on large purchases.

Retailers have the right to return only faulty records. Payments to the distribution companies for supplies of records should generally be effected within thirty days of the date of delivery. The largest distribution company, GDC, demands in addition that each customer place an order to the value of Sw.Cr. 25,000 upon establishing trading relations and later purchase records at the rate of Sw.Cr. 25,000 a year in order to gain the favours of GDC. Retailers unable to meet such demands are politely referred to the rack firms.

A relatively small proportion of record distribution occurs via public libraries. Seventyfive of Sweden's local authorities offer some kind of record service via their libraries, the nature of the service varying from one library to another. Normally it is possible to listen to records at the library as well as to borrow them. In 1976 there were in Sweden's libraries 370,000 music records, half of them with Western art music. Most libraries order their records from Bibliotekstjänst (Library Services) which via its "AV booklets" offers a selection of records to libraries. The number of records available in this way in 1977 was around 850, and in the same year the sales volume of Bibliotekstjänst totalled 37,000 records and music cassettes. In the sound recording field as a whole the services offered by libraries are, these days, of little importance.

7. The Reception and Usage of Records

Owning Records and Listening to Records

This section is based on the findings of a study conducted by the Audience and Program Research Department of the Swedish Broadcasting Corporation (SR/PUB) in collaboration with the sound recordings group of the National Council for Cultural Affairs in March 1977. Most of the results are from 1976. Comparisons have been made between 1970 and 1976, the figures for 1970 having been gathered from a number of sources by SR/PUB. The finding of this investigation apply to the whole of Sweden's population between 9 and 79 years of age.

In 1976 63 percent of households had some kind of record player, 14 percent having two or more record-players, 52 percent of households had a cassette recorder, 17 percent two or more cassette recorders. Most Swedes thus had access in the home to playback machines for sound recordings.

The total number of records in Sweden in 1976 was about 100 million, i.e., about 35 records per household. The most records were to be found in households with children and young people, elderly people seldom possessing records.

Table 8 shows that the time spent by Swedes listening to their own records at home increased by 400 percent between 1970 and 1976. If the time spent thus is added to the time spent listening to records on the radio (around 80 minutes per person per day) then an average of around 113 minutes each day or 680 hours per year are spent by the Swede in listening to records.

Table 8. *Record Listening and Cassette Listening in 1970 and 1976 (Minutes/Day/ Person, Hours/Year/Person and Total in Millions of Hours)*

	Mins./person/ day		Hours/person/ year		Total in millions of hours	
	1970	1976	1970	1976	1970	1976
Record listening	9	18	55	110	385	770
Cassette listening	–	15	–	90	–	630
Total	9	33	55	200	385	1,400

Source: SR/PUB

A comparison of the consumer patterns in various mass media (Table 9) shows that the share of total consumption of mass media on records has increased 7.3 percent between 1970 and 1976. During the same period radio listening has decreased by 8.5 percent. These figures must be interpreted as representing a gradual shift in the habits of Swedes from radio listening to listening to one's own records. One reason for this shift is

Table 9. *Mass Media Consumption in 1970 and 1976 (Minutes/Person/Day, Hours/Person/Year, Total in Millions of Hours Plus Share of Total Consumption)*

Medium	Mins./ person/day		Hours/ person/year		Total in millions of hours		Share of total con- sumption	
	1970	1976	1970	1976	1970	1976	1970	1976
Dailies	35	35	215	215	1,500	1,500	12.3	11.3
Radio	125	110	760	670	5,320	4,690	43.7	35.2
TV	95	114	580	690	4,060	4,830	33.4	36.3
Records	9	18	55	110	385	770	3.2	5.8
Cassettes	–	15	–	90	–	630	–	4.7
Film	1	1	6.5	5.5	45	40	0.4	0.3
Periodicals	(20)	(20)	(120)	(120)	(840)	(840)	6.9	6.3
Total	285	313	1,736.5	1,900.5	12,150	13,300	99.9	99.9

Source: SR/PUB

presumably the introduction of the cassette recorder, which makes it possible to record music from the radio.

Table 10 shows that record listening occupies a great deal of time for individuals between the ages of 9 to 24 who listen to their own records for an average of one hour a day. This group also listens to records on the radio for about an hour a day, giving a total average of two hours per person per day spent listening to records. Thus, many young people spend a substantial part of their leisure time listening to records.

A report published in 1975 by Rikskonserter (G. Nylöf: Swedish Youth – Their Attitudes to and Contacts with Music) shows that record listening was by far the most normal way for young people to encounter

Table 10. *Record Listening and Cassette Listening in 1976 for Various Age Groups (Minutes/Person/Day)*

Age group	Records	Cassettes	Total
9 – 14 years of age	27	31	58
15 – 24 years of age	33	27	60
25 – 44 years of age	23	17	40
45 – 54 years of age	14	11	25
55 – 64 years of age	8	5	13
65 – 79 years of age	3	2	5

music. The same study shows that 95 percent of all individuals between the ages of 12 and 24 are interested in music – a figure higher than any other area of interest.

Yet only a small percentage of schoolchildren consider music an interesting subject at school. Their great interest in music is cultivated for the most part during their leisure hours and in this context record listening is the most common form of contact with music. On the basis of these figures it may be asserted that the contents of records made available for consumption by young people play a major role in shaping their consciousness and patterns of music consumption.

In the lowest age group cassette listening is the most popular while time allotted to record listening increases along with the age of the listener. Thus, the new type of record, the cassette, has been accepted most rapidly by the youngest consumers.

Table 11 shows how record listening is distributed among various repertoire categories. This distribution in the proportion of total listening shows a similar pattern in all age groups. The amount of listening to children's records would certainly have been greater if children under nine years of age had been covered by the investigation.

Table 11. *Time Spent Listening to Sound Recordings in 1976, Classified in Various Repertoire Categories Plus Share of Total Listening*

Repertoire category	Minutes/person/week	Share of total listening %
Western art music	16	7
Folk music, ballads	18	8
Jazz, blues	12	5
Religious songs	11	5
Pop music	79	34
Dance music and other popular music	70	30
Children's records	9	4
Others	16	7

Source: SR/PUB

A number of observations may be made with the aid of Table 12.

The proportion of sales enjoyed by pop and dance music is appreciably greater than its share of either record listening time or musical interest: this lends support to the assertion that this type of music has a relatively brief period of popularity. The large sales volume can be explained by the fact that the record companies, via their marketing manage to give the

Table 12. *The Share Enjoyed by Various Repertoire Categories of Total Record Listening, of Sales Plus Interest Showed in Different Kinds of Music in Sweden in 1976*

Repertoire category	Share of record listening %	Share of sales %	Swedes who are very interested %
Western art music	7	6	23
Folkmusic, ballads	8	2	18
Jazz, blues	5	1	14
Religious songs	5	3	7
Pop music, dance music	64	78	52
Children's songs	4	5	–
Others	7	3	17
Total	100	100	131[1]

[1] This sum exceeds 100 since the same person can be very interested in more than one repertoire category.

Source: SR/PUB, Swedish Price and Cartel Board

impression that these records possess a higher level of utility than is in fact the case.

Both folk music and jazz have a much higher share of record listening than of sales, which shows that products in these categories, on average, have a much longer life than pop music and dance music. It also suggests a lack of folk music and jazz records. The time spent listening to music in these categories is proportional to the interest shown in the music.

The share of listening time enjoyed by Western art music is more or less equal to its share of sales. The level of interest in art music, however, is higher than indicated by purchases of, and time spent listening to, records: this confirms other impressions of music appreciation habits showing that those interested in art music indulge their interest to a greater extent than other music lovers by attending concerts and performances of musical theatre and also by playing themselves.

The Use and Functions of Records

It was stated in Chapter 2 that little research has been conducted into the use and functions of records. The use of records is part of a complicated pattern dependent on a number of conditions. This pattern was outlined by Göran Nylöf in 1977 in an essay on the need, or lack of need, for music policies concerned with pop music. The following excerpt from that essay shows patterns of music use suggesting various ways in which records can be of importance:

Music: Means of Communication or Product for Consumption?

If music is intended as a means of communication, this must have certain implications. For example:

— that some kind of musical activity (composing, performing, listening) is central to musical interests,
— that the effects of the music are based primarily on an inherent message or meaning: that which is expressed, or those associations which arise, contribute to the recipient's estimation of the music,
— that values with a long lifespan are sought, e.g. enduring experiences.

If music is intended as a product for consumption this must also have certain implications. For example:

— that most of the interest is concentrated on the finished product (the work, record, or concert);
— that the effect's of the music are based primarily upon qualities inherent in the music itself: how the music sounds and levels of achievement and effectivity contribute to the recipient's estimation of the music;
— that short-lived values, e.g. experiences for the moment, are regarded as sufficient.

People as musical beings are not orientated exclusively toward either communication or consumption, but their social background and affiliation to various groups and classes determines which type of orientation becomes dominant.

A person's working environment affects his or her leisure and other habits in many ways. A dull and monotonous job is often followed by a dull and monotonous leisure situation. A job which offers variety and independence helps to develop the resources of the person doing it, thus facilitating a deeper involvement and higher level of activity both in the field of culture and in other facets of life outside work. It is highly probable that a recipient role at work is conductive to a voluntarily recipient role outside work. Thus persons with subordinate roles at work ought to a great extent to become consumers of music rather than users of music as a means of communication. Persons engaged in mechanical, assembly-line tasks may on similar grounds be expected to exhibit a higher orientation towards consumption when it comes to music than those who are in their day-to-day work engaged in decision-making, the formulation of initiatives and creative activities.

The chances of drifting into passivity or routine musical habits are higher among consumption-orientated than among communication-orientated persons. Those equipped to participate in a mutual exchange, rather than merely to serve as a recipient in the musical process of communication, have a greater chance of developing musical habits with a high degree of involvement. Those able to express themselves musically may also be assumed to play a more active role in the search for new musical experiences and may be better prepared to overcome potential obstacles in the way of musical contacts. If the possibilities of bringing about a mutual musical exchange are limited or nonexistent, then the risk of easy-access music attaining dominance increases, often leading to apathy and passivity. This does not imply that orientation toward consumption necessarily excludes involvement, nor that an orientation toward communication in music guarantees involvement.

Private individuals do not arbitrarily decide the way in which they make use of music. Certain forces within our society encourage an orientation toward consumption and its resultant orientation toward production in the field of music. A high level of industrialization with large-scale production resulting in specialization, a well-developed market economy in a commercial system, an extensive mass communication network: all of these serve to suggest ways in which it is possible to reinforce an attitude interpreting music as a commodity to be bought and consumed. The mass production of music – as sheet music, records, etc. – is also a contributing factor to the realms of creation and performance.

Records may be used both as a means of communication and as a product for consumption. In the first case the record is most often a component necessary to a process – i.e. the record is used in a primary manner. In the second case the record is often an unnecessary side-issue in a process in which other phenomena and activities are more important – i.e. the record is used in a secondary manner.

Various forms of active listening, learning and information processes are ways of using records in a primary manner. Background music and the more-or-less continual music programs afforded by the radio come under the category of the use of music in a secondary manner. A special form of secondary use is the made-to-measure manipulative music used to increase either the output at a workplace or the sales in a department store.

Records are of great importance in shaping the consciousness of young people: they often use music records to show that they belong to a particular group or to identify themselves with various recording artists. The range of records made available to children is of great importance in influencing their conception of the world and their values in general as adults.

Sociological research shows that the contacts young people have had with music during the last ten years have acquired an increasingly one-sided emphasis upon certain types of pop, especially "disco music" and "hard rock" which are produced by the commercial record companies. These commercial companies use their marketing resources to woo young people into consuming such music. Their schools have failed to channel their great interest for music and records into areas offering greater prospects for self-fulfillment: one way of doing this would be to allow pupils to record their own records in some kind of media workshop.

A particular problem is posed by the relationship between live music and music on records: during the twentieth century recorded music has replaced live music in numerous contexts, but has also inspired people to music-making of their own and helped to spread different kinds of music. Developments in recording technology have resulted in recorded music these days becoming more and more a special kind of music which cannot be performed live. It is important to take action against the tendency for live music to be controlled or absorbed by recorded music. Recorded music and live music ought to be regarded as two separate ways of making music, each with a worth of its own. Cultural policies should be formulated with the aim of helping the two interplay and complement one another.

Wolfgang Arming

Economic Aspects of the Phonographic Industry
(Excerpt)

We all know that the phonographic industry is in a state of change at present. For the first time since the war growth rates have not met expectations, costs have risen and profits have sunk to an all-time low or even turned into deficits.

The economic problems which preoccupy us and give us many a headache, have, of course, not come about suddenly, but they were drowned by a lot of professional noise (noise-making is, after all, part of our job). Flops were hushed up, and it was mentioned that some projects had a turnover of millions. Gold and platin discs were awarded with glamour and publicity. Certainly, the phonographic industry was, and to my mind still is, an expanding field. In 1950, world-wide record sales in the Western hemisphere amounted to about 1 billion German Marks. In 1978 the proud figure of 23 billion Marks was reached, constituting an increase by more than 20 times – and that is certainly something to be proud of. Over the past 28 years, there has also been a marked shift in shares per continent.

1950	1978
1 billion	23 billion
80% U.S.A.	40% U.S.A.
10% Europe	35% Europe
5% Japan	13% Japan
5% rest of the world	7% South America
	2% Australia
	2% Africa
	1% rest

Although the phonographic industry surpassed the film industry in 1978, the economic dimensions remain rather modest. As mentioned before, world-wide sales amounted to 23 billion Marks, out of which the Federal Republic of Germany reached just about 2 billions.

Regarding private spending, we certainly do not reach a very high percentage, neither when viewed against other cultural items such as books, nor when compared with other industries trying, like we do, to "brighten" the monotony of our daily lives:

phonograms	0.27% of private spending
books	0.51%
hairdresser	0.67%
flowers	0.84% (Germany 1976)

We also take up very little of people's leisure time. About 16% play one record or cassette per day, 40% per week, and 51% per month.

It should be mentioned here that the 13 – 17 year-olds play twice as many records as the average person would.

Let us not forget, however, that the actual substance of our product, i.e. music, reaches the "consumer" also through radio, television, and the concert.

And I should like to point out in this context that the radio stations would be in no position to broadcast such an interesting and "in-expensive" programme, if our industry did not provide the music. The phonographic industry and radio/television therefore form an inevitable kind of symbiosis.

Prices

Are record and cassette prices really too high? I personally do not think so – the European average (not considering the price developments over the past few weeks) shows that prices for our products have dropped considerably, or, taking inflation into account, amount to only 30% of 1967.

20 years ago, a factory worker in the Federal Republic of Germany had to work well over 20 minutes to buy 60 seconds of music. 10 years ago, the figure was 10 minutes, and in 1978 75 seconds. This relation clearly shows how cheap, or rather inexpensive records have become. Of course, we sell a lot more these days.

Like all other industries, we too had to face cost increases; we have, however, not passed the increased cost on to the consumer. The fact that we have remained competitive and economically sound despite keen competition, is mainly the result of continuous streamlining in the factories and offices, but also because of the positive reactions on the part of our audience. The growth rates amounting to 15 and more percent have recently stopped, resulting in a sudden, vehement, world-wide economic crisis.

As already mentioned, it is our task to make music – as an important pillar of culture – accessible to everyone, without, however, requesting or receiving any Government subsidies normally granted to other cultural fields (we have no value-added-tax advantage, for example).

Thus the paradoxical situation arises where the legislator does actually give preferential VAT treatment to the creators of our products, i.e. the authors and artists, but not to the record industry who try to disseminate these cultural assets by means of soundcarriers. The cultural aspect gets lost in this process, says the law; the musical score of Beethoven's Fifth Symphony is, to be sure, part of our cultural heritage; the very same symphony conducted by Böhm or Karajan is not?

Who then, besides the Government, profits from a record? The costs for a record can roughly be broken down as follows: One third remains with the trade, the retailer; another third goes to the music-makers, i.e. the artists, composers, and performers in the studio; and one third remains with the industry and is used up by distribution, administration, advertising and promotion. Naturally, these average values differ, depending on the country and the record produced.

Let me illustrate the split of costs by means of two extreme examples, i.e. two fictitious record companies, one in the U.S.A. and one in Austria.

U.S.A.: In order to make a modest profit in the United States, the turnover must reach about 133 million dollars. This corresponds to an invoiced net turnover of 101,322,000 dollars. America, like England, belongs to the international sources of pop-repertoire, therefore investments in the field of music are higher than in other countries. The share of our fictitious company in the music costs[1] is correspondingly higher and amounts to about 35%. On the other hand, the so-called administrative expenses, i.e. the manufacturing price of the records, and the costs for covers and albums, which are fairly low because of the large circulation, can be assumed at about 26%.

In *Austria*, a company must have a turnover of about 56 million Austrian Schillings in order to survive. This corresponds to an invoiced net turnover of about 45.2 million Austrian Schillings. Austria is not exactly considered a source of commercial pop repertory, and investments in the field of music are therefore comparatively low: about 21% of the net turnover. The so-called administrative expenses are rather high, about 41 – 42%, brought about by the small circulation.

Let us have another look at the distribution of costs. The trade receives a fixed third. The music costs have risen in the course of the years, recording and royalties have spiralled. Manufacturing costs for phono-

---

[1] Music-cost: direct and indirect recording expenses, studio, royalties, guarantees etc.

grams have varied greatly over the past 5 – 6 years. Singles have become more expensive; the reasons were mainly increases in personnel costs. In the mid-seventies, streamlining in the manufacturing process had reached its peak. Cost increases with LP's were somewhat below the singles because pressing could be streamlined more effectively. As to administration, the increase in personnel costs could also be checked by means of automation. However, the alarming rise in music costs has left its imprints on our industry. There has been a steep upward trend over the past decades. The reasons are as follows:

First, artists and producers have increased their demands decisively; second, royalties have doubled over the last years; third, the guarantees of the well-established artists, have reached six-digit sums within the past 5 years. In addition to this, there are the increased production and studio equipment costs. This cost explosion, especially in the music sector, could only be counteracted by steadily increasing sales. The decisive factor was that some few records reached all-time record sales, e.g.

Saturday Night Fever
Grease

These "Mega-Sellers" have, at least superficially, made up for the sharp cost increases.

All responsible managers in the music industry have realized that excessive demands on the part of the producers and artists must and cannot be met readily since this would endanger the very existence of the record companies.

Furthermore artists, publishers, record companies lose millions of dollars through piracy – what I would like to call the "cancer of the music business".

In addition to this we have the millions of blank cassettes for home-taping, which is bound to have a detrimental effect on the sale of records and cassettes.

Our industry may face a stern test in the coming years in the forms of a stagnate market, increasing costs, piracy and home-taping prevailing.

To date, there exists no sufficient law that protects the artists' creative properties and this serious situation is the cause of decreasing revenues too.

In any case, we have a two-fold responsibility to protect not only that part of our business which is the documentation of music, our cultural function, but also, in the economic sense, to bring music to the people through the principle of industrial management.

Our socio-political task is to meet the demands of the market and maintain the existence of the company, to give employees job security, thus avoiding unemployment.

Luigi Del Grosso Destreri and Cleto Corposanto

Production and Consumption of Phonograms in Italy: In Search of the Sources of Research

1. Introduction

To give a general view of the statistical sources relating to the production and consumption of phonograms in Italy is a thorny task for the researcher. The institute which ought to be the principal source, the S.I.A.E. – Società Italiana degli Autori ed Editori (Italian Society of Authors and Publishers), is found to be rather unreliable, as it offers no information whatsoever about records imported from abroad and, which is even more serious, does not list the so-called "public domain works" (i.e., works that are no longer subject to author's rights), which account for an enormous share of the market, primarily in the field of classical music, but also in the light music sector (evergreens).

Another source should be the A.F.I. – Associazione dei Fonografici Italiani (a manufacturers' association belonging to the IFPI); but it includes only the major Italian producers. The information furnished by this association is bound to be incomplete, as it does not even cover all the producers affiliated to it.

Finally, there is another type of sources represented by the public opinion polls conducted in Italy by various research institutes. This data derives from the statements of persons questioned about the number of records, cassettes and other phonograms they have bought. Though merely by induction, these figures obviously include the purchases of illicit products brought onto the market in violation of the law, and, as we shall see later on, they constitute the most reliable source of information about our country.

Before presenting the data we collected and assessing its reliability, it seems appropriate to draw a picture of the legal situation in Italy, as reflected in the laws relating to the production and sale of phonograms.

2. The Legal Situation in Italy

When, at the beginning of our century, the first devices for the mechanical reproduction of sound appeared in several countries, copyright in Italy was subject to the Act of September 19, 1882, No. 1012, which ensured to the "authors of intellectual creations" the exclusive right to publish and reproduce their works and to sell reproductions thereof. With respect to publication in print and the sale of printed copies the duration of copyright protection was divided into two terms:

a) the initial copyright term, which was of an exclusive nature, extended throughout the author's life and after his death over the first 40 years from the publication of the work;

b) the second term can be described as "public domain subject to a tax" in the sense that reproduction and sale became free, on condition of payment to the author for another 40 years.

For performing rights, on the other hand, the term was 80 years from the date of first publication.

In 1886 Italy signed the Bern Convention, which stated that the manufacture and sale of instruments designed for sound reproduction did not constitute a case of musical imitation.

A new Copyright Act (No. 1950, November 7, 1925) was passed in 1925, which stipulated that exclusive rights in a work should subsist for a single period of 50 years after the author's death. "Public domain subject to a tax" (Point b of the 1882 Act) was repealed.

In 1926 the S.I.D.E., Società Incassi Diritti Editoriali – a collecting society – was formed, which later become S.E.D.R.I.M. – Società Esercizio Diritti Riproduzione Meccanica. In 1929, this society together with similar French and German societies, founded the B.I.E.M. – Bureau International de l'Edition Mécanique, to safeguard international protection of copyright owners[1]. After the dissolution of S.E.D.R.I.M. its functions were taken over by the S.I.A.E. in 1970.

In the statutes of the S.I.A.E., as amended in 1974, it is laid down that "the rights protected by its various departments in the works assigned to them, include those relating to mechanical reproduction"[2].

The act which still protects these rights dates from April 22, 1941 (No. 633) and refers to literary and musical creations etc., including musical works and compositions as well as variations. The rights in these works, more specifically the exclusive right of publication and economic utilization of any kind, be it original or derived, belong to the authors. In

---

[1] For a more complete treatment of the matter refer to S.E.D.R.I.M. ed., *Il diritto di riproduzione meccanica e la relativa amministrazione*, publication of S.E.D.R.I.M, Milan 1968.

[2] Cf. S.I.A.E, ed., *La pirateria discografica*, S.I.A.E., Rome 1977.

addition to these rights the act also protects the so-called "related rights" connected with the exercise of the copyright, including those held by the manufacturer of the gramophone record or any other device for sound reproduction. The manufacturer has the exclusive right to copy, by means of any duplicating procedure, the mentioned record or device of his own production and to put it up for sale.

We ought to recall that the act of 1925 abolished the "public domain subject to a tax" and provided for a single copyright term of 50 years after the author's death. It was only a question of a "public domain": although the pertinent act from 1941 provides for fees due to the state for "each and every performance or radio transmission", it makes no reference whatsoever to the mechanical reproduction of public domain works, which are, therefore, not subject to such dues[3].

The manufacture of phonograms reproducing public domain works is, therefore, not subject to any control from the part of S.I.A.E. And yet, these works make up a most significant part of the phonograms sold on the market, about which no statistical source can give us any definite (non-inductive) information.

One might think that the protection of artists' or performers' rights could help us to make an estimate of this market. But the law only provides for their remuneration by those who utilize their creations or performances in any form different from the authorized one. It is true that the Rome Convention of October 10, 1961 (ratified by Italy in 1973) has modified this situation by giving performers the right to object against the recording of their performances and against the reproduction or radio transmission of authorized recordings, but as yet no penal provision has been issued for the protection of those rights. Though singers and musicians are entitled to equitable rates of compensation for the non-private use of their records, they cannot oppose such use and have, therefore, no negotiatory power when it comes to the settling of terms.

In accordance with the provisions of the 1961 Convention, the "Istituto Mutualistico Assistenza Interpreti ed Esecutori Musicali" (Mutual Assistance Institute of Musical Interpreters and Performers) was set up in Rome in 1979, with the support of the Federazione Unitaria dei Lavoratori dello Spettacolo (Union of Stage Workers).

The Institute will be in charge of collecting and administrating such compensations. Since this trade-union organization has been founded so recently, it is impossible to predict its potential value as a reliable source of statistical data about the utilization of phonograms.

Turning to the problem of "public domain", we conclude that: the official body in charge of collecting data on the production of phono-

---

[3] Ibid.

grams has no information to offer, institutionally, about this important sector of production.

This is a first, conspicuous, statistical "gap" which is actually a legal "gap". As we shall see in the next chapter, we are also faced with shortcomings of an "illegal" nature.

3. Market Typology

We take a summary look at the types of products sold on the Italian market, comparing legal and illegal ones.

a) Legitimately Produced Records, Musicassettes and Cartridges

    a1) regularly produced material (certified with S.I.A.E. stamp);
    a2) legitimately produced material without certification:
        i) produced before 1971 (records and musicassettes) or in 1972. (cartridges);
        ii) produced abroad and regularly imported;
        iii) containing only compositions that have passed into the public domain or are by authors not protected by the S.I.A.E.

At this point we have to make two observations. It is true that the S.I.A.E. can protect the rights of members without being expressly authorized to do so, but it is not obligatory for authors to become members of the S.I.A.E. (this, we believe, is an observation of little statistical significance). Much more important is the importation of phonograms, particularly in those cases in which the reseller has to pay the customs fees directly, without being in any way obliged to supply the quantitative data to an official body. Imports, therefore, remain another sector of the Italian market on which it appears impossible to obtain definite statistical data. But let us move on to the clandestine market:

b) Illicitly Produced Records, Musicassettes and Cartridges

    b1) complete counterfeits bearing falsified S.I.A.E. stamp;
    b2) products without S.I.A.E. stamp:
        i) counterfeits of trademarks only, with phantasy marks or without marks;
        ii) of foreign production, imported without permission[4].

There is an office within the S.I.A.E. which is in charge of dealing with what the S.I.A.E. defines in its publications as "phonogram piracy"; but

---

[4] For the cited categories refer to S.I.A.E., ed., *La pirateria discografica*, S.I.A.E., Rome 1978.

we shall soon see that very little is known about this market and that all estimates are extremely vague, especially in relation to the overall projection we are going to make, based on the data derived from public opinion polls.

In a study published in 1978[5] the S.I.A.E. states that the major centres of clandestine production are Naples, Milan, Bergamo, Bologna and Turin. 36 clandestine manufacturing plants were closed down in 1977. The estimates given with respect to the clandestine market are solely based on the production capacity of the discovered plants: "The calculation, based as it is on the capacity of the clandestine plants known to the S.I.A.E., is necessarily incorrect due to the lack of data." The figure given for complete counterfeits is 2,500,000, for illicit products 4,500,000. The economic damage would be little less than 15,000 million lire in terms of production plus a loss of more than 1,500 million in royalties.

Another possible consideration concerns the production of blank tapes in Italy. For its estimate the S.I.A.E. does not refer to official data from the industry and the ministries but to an enquiry published in a weekly ("L'Espresso" of May 21, 1978). We quote the precise wording: "The annual proceeds of sales of blank tapes in Italy plausibly amount to 20,000 million lire. If one considers that the national production of musicassettes, referred to the year 1977, is about 12 million pieces (including works in stock, not yet copyrighted, public domain works or works not protected by the S.I.A.E.), which corresponds to about 2,500 million of the mentioned sales, it can be inferred that this production would account for not quite one eighth of the tapes, while the remaining seven eighth would be designated for educational, professional or illicit as well as legitimate private use." These statements are alarming as they imply statistics in which logic has no place. First of all, one concludes that in Italy seven eighth of the blank tapes sold would amount to an easy 96 million pieces! An absurd figure which also contradicts the very estimates earlier made by the S.I.A.E. Besides, a sales figure (20,000 million) referring to blank tapes is compared with another sales figure (2,500 million) referring to recorded tapes. From the relation between two incommensurable quantities one deduces the unrealistic figure of 96 million pieces. While, on the contrary, it is most probable that the figures given by "L'Espresso" refer to the national production of blank tapes (12 million), because, as we shall see later on, this figure corresponds with the results of the opinion poll, which gives an estimate of about 25 million tapes per annum. About 50% of the tapes purchased in Italy are presumably imported.

---

[5] Op. cit., 1978.

4. Statistical Sources

We believe that for a correct and comprehensive approach to a study of statistical sources relating to the production and consumption of phonograms in Italy (but obviously the observation is also valid for any other country), one must not neglect the aspects of so-called "micro" and "macro" data. Though it has been proved that the results of these two types of inquiries are not comparable for purely technical reasons, we think it expedient to point out the differences existing at the level of data analysis, and to underline the current trends in our country.

As is known, data collected at the macro-sociological level principally permits comparisons in time and space.

It goes without saying that this is certainly a step forward towards the knowledge — acquired with the help of data derived from opinion polls — of percentages of these very data, from which one can infer collective behaviour patterns. But "... unfortunately those responsible rarely know about it ..."[6].

This, however, is not the only advantage derived from the availability of data collected at the macro rather than the micro level. It is not only true that it is possible to work with the so-called "historical series"; there are at least two other additional very interesting aspects that derive from the use of such types of data.

We refer primarily to the possibility of carrying out multivariate statistical analyses (to which we shall refer later on), and secondly to the availability of "social indicators", which would help to understand the phenomenon in its entire complexity. Over the past years, a lively debate has developed about the concept of "social indicator".

From among the many definitions we have selected K. Land's:

"I propose that the term *social indicators* refers to social statistics that:

a) are components in a social system model (including sociopsychological, economic, demographic and ecological) or of some particular segment or process thereof;

b) can be collected and analyzed at various times and accumulated into a time-series;

c) can be aggregated or disaggregated to levels appropriate to the specifications of the model.

By social system model I mean a conception of social processes which is formulated verbally, logically, mathematically or in terms of computer simulation. The important point is that the criterion for classifying

---

[6] Cf. Beaud, P., *Methodologische Probleme*. In: Blaukopf, K., *Massenmedium Schallplatte*, Breitkopf & Härtel, Wiesbaden 1977, pp. 66 – 87.

social statistics as a social indicator is its *information value* derived from its empirically verified nexus in a conceptualization of a social process"[7].

From the above it seems sufficiently clear that the use of social indicators becomes of crucial importance for the understanding and explanation of phenomena like the production and consumption of phonograms in a certain country, in the sense that these phenomena will not be interpreted out of the overall social, economic and cultural context.

A different, but in our view equally useful consideration refers to the possibility of analyzing the data by means of multivariate statistical analyses. In fact, as one can easily see, it seems a rather thorny task to explain how consumption and production of phonograms vary in time and space on the basis of one single variable, whatever that variable may be; whereas the theory that it is possible to analyze the total variation of such data, departing from a set of independent, explicative variables, appears much better founded.

No matter, whether one is considering the possibility of using methods of multivariate statistical analysis or of being able to define a series of social indicators in the field of production and consumption of phonograms, one must never exclude these issues from considerations of a methodological nature.

For instance, the choice of a territorial unit will, apart from representing a socio-political problem, certainly not be unrelated to the possibility of applying certain statistical methods and to the interpretation of results.

In the case of Italy, for example, our previous inquiries, conducted at the macro-sociological level about the so-called "cultural consumption" of the Italians[8] (from which phonograms were necessarily excluded for lack of data), brought as first and intermediate result the identification of the province as the most reliable territorial unit of analysis.

The subsequent stages of research were, therefore, based on the data collected in the 95 Italian provinces, which permitted, first, the identification of two "factors" called "mass" cultural consumption (with the

---

[7] Cf. Land, K., On the definition of social indicators. In: *The American Sociologist*, 1971, vol. 6, pp. 322 – 325.

[8] Research into "cultural consumption" of the Italians was conducted by a group of professors from the Department of Socialisation at the Sociological Faculty of the Libera Università degli Studi in Trent.

consumption of movies, variety shows etc., as saturated variables)[9] and "elite" cultural consumption (with theatre, concert and opera performances as saturated variables)[10]; secondly, it permitted the categorization of the 95 provinces into four homogeneous areas, which replace the by now obsolete division of the territory into North, Centre and South, and the somewhat less obsolete, but still erroneous regional classification[11].

---

[9] The term "saturated" is directly derived from the technique of multivariate statistical analysis used in this case, that is to say from the so-called "factor analysis". The principal aim of this analysis, used, as it were, on the "explorative" level, may be summarized as the reduction of a certain number of "manifest" variables related to a smaller number of "latent" variables: such a procedure must by no means lead to a loss of information. The "factors" manifest themselves as the synthesis of a certain number of variables, which at the same time can serve to identify their possible specific character. During a stage following upon the one we defined as explorative, these factors can be used in place of the set of variables, in order to evidence the socio-statistical relations between the variables. Thus, we say that a variable is "saturated" with respect to a certain factor, if it is possible to assign to this factor a significantly great relevance for its overall variability.

[10] A subdivision of territorial observation units according to the factors of "high" and "low" cultural consumption can be summed up in the following table, which gives in four fields the respective numbers of Italian provinces characterized by a particular situation:

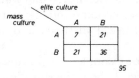

[11] In this case the technique of multivariate analysis is the one known as *discriminant analysis*; as before, we briefly recall the main objectives.

In the course of sociological research, the researcher is very often faced with the question of how to classify an entity of statistical observation units (no matter whether they be objects, territorial units etc.), grouping them in categories, which related to a common group of variables, should be as "different" as possible from one another: categories that express the conditions of homogeneity "within" and heterogeneity "among" better than any other (the terms are borrowed from the better known variance analysis).

The discriminant analysis serves to solve such problems from a dual perspective: as soon as the observation units have been grouped into categories, it may be interesting to reach the point of identifying the pattern of variables that will better define them (classification analysis); on the other hand, again departing from the grouping of units into categories, the crucial moment of the discriminant analysis is that of verifying how such categories remain "coherent" — estimating the percentages of possible discrepancies between "a priori" and "a posteriori" assignments — with respect to a previously fixed entity of variables.

We have just pointed out that it has been impossible to introduce into such studies data related to the consumption of phonograms, for the simple reason that no such data is available, even if indirectly observable. We have already said that the body responsible for collecting and distributing such data in Italy is the S.I.A.E., but it happens that the enormous shortcomings of the data supplied by that body are revealed even upon a cursory analysis.

5. Existing Data

We shall try to clarify the point by giving some examples; as far as data is concerned, we take 1977 as the "latest year of reference"; but in qualitative terms the study is valid for any year. One of our major problems is the total lack of data about the consumption of phonograms, broken down according to zones; the only data available refers to the entire country.

It goes without saying that the national consumption is far from homogeneous; under such conditions it seems most problematic to attempt an interpretation of this consumption, departing from other factors to which it is, no doubt, related.

Another serious shortcoming relates to the import/export figures: the consumption of phonograms indicated by the S.I.A.E. includes export figures. But no indication is given as to the import figures; ony may surmise that the latter are higher than the former, but quite obviously one cannot base a statistical analysis on such surmises.

In the light of these limitations, the data we are going to give further on is far from being completely reliable. Still, we shall go ahead with some preliminary observations.

The data furnished by the S.I.A.E. excludes the consumption of phonograms with works that have passed into the public domain; but the production and consumption of such phonograms is quite considerable, particularly as far as classical music is concerned (which brings us to still another point: there exists only an all-inclusive figure, while no figures are available about the consumption of classical music, light music etc., that is to say broken down according to musical genres).

It seems appropriate to point to still another phenomenon of great quantitative importance. In Italy we have for some time had record companies specializing in low-price products. The catalogues of these companies have always offered records at medium and low prices. Initially, they offered series like "Joker" (SAAR) and "Penny" (RIFI), mostly purchased en bloc from abroad and sold at unusual points of sale (department stores, kiosks, etc.).

In June 1976, the RCA launched "Lineatre" (a medium-priced series, originally at L 3,000, now at L 3,500, compared with 7/8000 normally paid for a record). The catalogue is not composed of old hits that could not be sold at full price, but of an absolutely normal repertoire, which is supposed to be able to reach the sales level of at least 5,000 copies.

According to data issued by the company, "Lineatre" sales amounted to over 10 million pieces (cf. "Musica e Dischi", No. 394, April 1979, p. 26) within two-and-a-half years, from June 1976 to April 1979. Records accounted for 50%, musicassettes for 40% and cartridges for 10%.

In terms of genres, jazz accounts for less than 4%, classical music for 15%, folk for between 15 and 20%, pop music for more than 60%.

Our estimate of public domain works is consequently not lower than one-and-a-half million pieces per year. In this context one must recall that a large share of the "public domain" market is held by songs, midway between folk and pop which have played a very important role in the musical culture of specific social configurations: a case in point are the "canzoni napoletane" (neapolitan songs), many of which are public domain works.

The proliferation of initiatives like "Lineatre" (for instance the "Record Bazar" of CGD which was set up in October 1976 and sold over half a million pieces[12] in 1978) is a useful indicator of a constantly growing market.

It seems superfluous to underline that this phenomenon, on which "Musica e Dischi" provides ample information, implicitly contradicts the quantitative data about the whole market supplied by the same journal and most probably derived from the S.I.A.E. data, which, as we shall see, grossly underestimates the real market.

From 1971 up to date, more than ten special journals have come into being, which are all quite profitable as they have no difficulty in selling their ad space. For this very reason some publishers (Publisuona di Roma) commissioned the first systematic inquiry into the musical interests and preferences of the Italians from Demoskopea. It is to this data that a serious journal like "Espansione" makes reference (in a report from January 1979) to illustrate the music market.

So it is all the more surprising that the President of AFI, in his speech at the Discoexpo meeting (trade fair of gramophone records) in which he, while quoting from the "Espansione" report, should use for a 1977 market estimate the very AFI data which we received and which, as we shall see further on, is not very reliable.

---

[12] Our estimate from the information published in "Musica e Dischi" No. 395, May 1979, p. 29.

In fact, this data "does not include the records produced for exportation and was obtained from a universe formed by 26 of 34 production companies selected for the purpose" (cf. letter from AFI of May 9, 1979, in the Appendix).

These 34 companies obviously do not constitute the universe – this time in the true sense of the word – of Italian production; of the 34 only 26 provided the requested data and no projection was made estimating the universe from such a biased "sample".

Before presenting the data supplied by the S.I.A.E., we ought to point out that for obvious reasons there is a lack of data about private production (of which little or nothing is known) and about clandestine production (in this case one can only develop rather vague theories).

Bearing this in mind, the data supplied by the S.I.A.E. about the consumption of phonograms in Italy in 1977 is the following:

45 r.p.m.	21,000,000
33 r.p.m. + extended	16,000,000
musicassettes	7,500,000
cartridges	2,000,000
Total	46,500,000

As can easily be inferred from what has been said above, this is evidently an underestimation of the actual figures; particularly with respect to the so-called "phonogram piracy" the S.I.A.E. supplies information which permits the assumption that, compared with the clandestine production of records, which is practically non-existent, the clandestine production of tapes and cassettes is almost equal to the official one: in numerical terms this would mean that of the about 18 million musicassettes and cartridges sold every year, half are coming from the "official", the other half from the clandestine market.

In spite of all the mentioned limitations, there remains the fact that the data furnished by the S.I.A.E. is the only basis on which studies and interpretations concerning the consumption of phonograms in our country are conducted.

Just for the sake of illustration we reproduce a diagram taken from a special journal[13] which is meant to demonstrate the development of the Italian production of recorded music from 1964 to 1977.

---

[13] Cf. the "Supplemento" to No. 384 of "Musica e Dischi" entitled *Il mercato del Disco in Italia* (*dal 1960 ai giorni nostri*). Cf. also Cane, G., *Il consumo della musica*, Armando, Rome 1975, in particular to pp. 61 – 69.

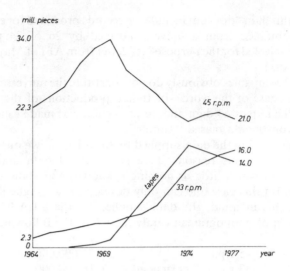

A simple comparison will show that the figures for 1977 appear to be those supplied by the S.I.A.E.[14]; consequently one may also assume that those for the previous years come from the same source.

An additional source of information could – and should – be the AFI (Associazione dei Fonografici Italiani); we use the potential mood, because just as in the case of the S.I.A.E. the data does not seem to be completely reliable.

In fact, an estimate furnished by the Association for 1977 shows certain limitations:

a) As mentioned above, the estimated figures refer to 26 of 34 production companies selected for the purpose.

b) It is mentioned that the data does not include the records produced for exportation, but no mention whatsoever is made of importations.

c) With respect to "public domain" works, the comment we made about the S.I.A.E. data applies also to that furnished by AFI.

A simple comparison of the data supplied by the Associazione dei Fonografici Italiani and that of the S.I.A.E. shows that the criteria for the data collection resemble those previously discussed.

The AFI data about the consumption of phonograms in Italy in 1977 is the following:

---

[14] The increase – compared with the S.I.A.E. data – in the consumption of tapes can be explained by the fact that the figure in "Musica e Dischi" includes an estimate of the clandestine market.

45 r.p.m.	17,796,206
33 r.p.m.	16,221,674
musicassettes	6,562,305
cartridges	1,185,646
special records	2,524,828

Total 44,290,659

Here again, the figures are not broken down according to musical genres nor is there any territorial subdivision.

In the note on sales of various musical genres, AFI, interestingly enough, makes reference to the report about sales increases in the journal "Musica e Dischi" of October 1978.

It follows that also this data has an exclusively indicative value, because no mention whatsoever is made of its sources. In any case, we learn that during the period 1967 – 1977 sales of Italian pop music show an abrupt rise by 390.6% (from about 16,000 to 62,500 million lire), compared with 486% for foreign pop music (from 10,700 to 52,000 million); the increase for classical music is shown to amount to 750% (from 2,000 to 15,000 million lire).

We have previously hinted at the interrelations between so-called "micro" and "macro" data, mentioning the necessity of being able to construct some indicators with a significant explicative potential within the framework of a macro-sociological study. In this connection it has also been mentioned that the selection of variables permitting a comprehensive and correct inquiry is not always easy. Here, sample inquiries may prove to be useful; in other words, "micro" studies may be a valid basis on which to build theories for analysis to be conducted at the "macro" level.

This is one of the reasons why we are now going to mention two comprehensive sample inquiries conducted by one of the most renowned research institutes in Italy, by Demoskopea, though we are principally mentioning them because they undoubtedly represent a point of sound methodological reference and are thus useful for the purpose of comparisons and reliable estimates.

The two inquiries, rather similar in qualitative terms, were carried out at an interval of a few months; the first one dates from June 1978, the second one refers to the first months of this year.

Thus we are concerned with recently collected data, supplied by a methodologically sound institute, and, therefore, a most valuable source of information.

The inquiry conducted between January and February 1979 was of the "omnibus" type[15], based on a questionnaire that contained a special chapter on music.

---

[15] This term is used to denote studies in which various corporations may participate and contribute to financially.

The sample was composed of about 2000 individuals from 15 years upwards[16], and the correspondence with the universe (more than 42,000,000 persons) was controlled by the usual variables such as sex, age, geographical region, size of the place of residence and social conditions; there were 145 sample points.

From the data obtained from the Demoskopea inquiry we have selected some tables which are given in the Appendix.

This data enables us to arrive at a new estimate of the consumption of phonograms in Italy, which, quite apart from the fact that it does not refer to the same periods as those mentioned above, clearly reveals profound differences which quite obviously are not referable to a market expansion but much rather confirm that we were justly perplexed by the data we obtained from S.I.A.E. and AFI.

From the replies given to the individual questions about the purchase of records, one can derive an average, weighted with the number of units purchased[17], for each type of phonogram and cassette. In the table below we give some values, which, when related to the universe underlying the questioned sample, provide an estimate of the phonogram market:

Average annual purchases of 33 r.p.m.	1.06
Average annual purchases of 45 r.p.m.	0.72
Average annual purchases of blank cassettes	0.59
Average annual purchases of recorded cassettes	0.91

We have to point out that these average values differ from those which one can find in the tables given in the Appendix; this is due to the fact that the latter are related to the sub-sample composed only of "purchasers" and the above figures are to estimate the overall Italian market.

The universe underlying the sample questioned by Demoskopea is composed of about 42,600,000 persons; in the light of the data just presented, it is now possible to arrive at the following estimate of the phonogram market in Italy for 1978:

33 r.p.m.	45,156,000
45 r.p.m.	30,672,000
recorded cassettes	38,766,000
blank cassettes	25,134,000
Total	139,728,000

---

[16] This is, no doubt, a limitation, though not a very serious one, as it excludes the consumption by the age group below 15: but, as we shall tell later on, it seems that the estimates that one can derive from them are nevertheless indicatively significant.

[17] Value 3 was assigned to the category of size 1 − 5; value 7.5 to that between 5 − 10, a.s.o.

It is evident that these figures differ profoundly from those previously given in this study (cf. ch. 3).

No doubt, these figures too, represent only estimates of the actual Italian market for recorded music; but the greater reliability guaranteed by the sample in contrast to the undeniable limitations of the previously mentioned data ensures that the estimates made on the basis of the results obtained from the Demoskopea inquiry may rightly be regarded as closer to the truth.

We shall, at this point, try to sum up the quantitative aspect of the situation prevailing with respect to phonogram statistics in Italy.

As repeatedly pointed out, the data furnished by specialized institutions (S.I.A.E., A.F.I.) are of very little potential value for explicative or projective ends; apart from the obvious considerations regarding the method of data collection, this is proved by a comparison with data coming from sample inquiries.

For the rest, we have already had occasion to show that the data, in order to be more than merely "descriptive", must be collected with due regard to certain characteristics.

6. Methodological Propositions

At this point we should like to sum up what has been said above in a number of propositions.

First of all, it seems of decisive importance to select a territorial observation unit for the collection of data and for analyses; in fact, we have already pointed out that it is most problematic to use data collected at the national level for possible statistical analyses.

Thus, it should be underlined that the selection of such an observation unit, which for Italy ought to be the individual province and for other countries may be a similar administrative region, must be made in a way permitting a comparison of data.

Coming back to the situation in Italy, it also appears indispensable for the data on consumption to be broken down not so much or not only according to the "duration" of the record (or the cassette), but rather according to "musical genres"; taking for granted a lack of homogeneity in the complex consumption data with respect to the individual zones under consideration, it can be assumed that there are additional differences with respect to the musical genres; one has to be aware that this is another variable that is interrelated with diverse "factors" characterizing different cultural situations.

For a study about the consumption of phonograms it will undoubtedly be necessary to solve the problem of how to obtain data about the "public domain" works, which, apart from their overall effect on the consumption data, almost certainly have also a decisive role to play in connection with the data about the individual musical genres.

Such a point of departure (i.e. data collected for individual territorial units and for musical genres) could provide the basis for research into explicative indicators, on the one hand, and, on the other hand, into the relations evidenced by statistical analyses which possibly exist between the data on the consumption of phonograms and others of a more or less general character (education, standard of living, etc.) which we believe one must not leave aside, if one wishes to take a comprehensive and correct approach to the problem of the consumption of recorded music in a country.

7. Quantitative and Qualitative Analysis

A subject, which is of particular concern to us and which ought to be at least briefly treated, is the interrelationship between quantitative and qualitative inquiries into the production of phonograms. Even if one arrived at reliable estimates – or definite data – about the production in the individual countries, one would still be far from having even an approximate idea of the world's cultural production centres. We feel, it is worth recalling that phonograms are "culture" in the widest anthropological sense of the term.

There are at least two aspects to the issue:

a) the import/export flow (which countries are dominating and which countries are "purchasers" or dependents and in what sense);

b) the distribution centres of cultural fashions (one will learn little about the way in which cultural fads spread in our contemporary world, if one simply examines the production data without knowing where certain styles originated and where they were taken up later, even if in a "tame" way).

We should like to refer to an earlier study conducted by one of the present authors[18]. It was concerned with four European countries – Italy, France, England and Hungary – and in addition to analyzing lyrics and music it also dealt with the import and export flow of hits. It must be mentioned that the songs were selected on the basis of "sales" (practically

---

[18] Cf. Del Grosso Destreri, L., *Aspetti della cultura giovanile di massa. Atteggiamenti e valori nelle 41 canzoni di maggior successo del 1967: una ricerca di analisi del contenuto.* In: "Ikon" No. 71, October – December 1969, pp. 105 – 142; id., *Atteggiamenti e valori nelle canzoni di successo in quattro paesi europei (1964 – 1967): analisi del contenuto e analisi musicale.* In: "Quaderni di Ikon", No. 12, 1970, pp. 37 – 72; id., *Europäisches Hit-Panorama. Erfolgsschlager in vier europäischen Ländern 1964 und 1967. Aussagen, Inhalte, Analysen,* G. Braun, Karlsruhe, 1972.

speaking: by checking the hit parades and correcting them with information obtained from the record companies; a method, which is not absolutely correct in scientific terms but adequate for a primarily qualitative analysis).

Following we give one of the tables[19]:

	Italy		France		England	
	1964	1967	1964	1967	1964	1967
Songs (total)	100	100	100	100	100	100
Translations %	44	34	82	27	62	28
From the USA	21	11	63	12	54	28
From Great Britain	3	17	16	12	–	–

Hungary is not included in the table, because there the dissemination of foreign songs was regulated by a central agency, which in practice meant the release of about one foreign hit per month. This failed to reflect the cultural climate in the country, as it disregarded the dissemination through hardly quantifiable radio transmissions, directly or indirectly financed by the United States, offering mainly western music. The data was commented as follows:

"The first observation refers to the general decrease in translations: England and France show a shift from a majority of translations to a majority of original songs. Even Italy follows this trend, though much less conspicuously. If the dominating foreign presence in Italy and France in 1964 was the United States, England vigorously conquered a good part of the market in 1967, surpassing American imports into Italy and moving up to the same level as France. But England imports almost exclusively from the United States (even if in 1967 the percentage dropped considerably): if, on the international level it remains to a certain degree dependent on the United States, on the European level England now holds the same rank as the USA."

When reading this last paragraph, we should remember that it referred to the importation and exportation *not* of phonograms in general but of hits only. This means that among the countries under consideration, the leader in the field of youth mass culture was undoubtedly the United States, the biggest exporter in the world, even if, in those years, England seemed to be the breeding ground of cultural innovation.

---

[19] Cf. Del Grosso Destreri, L., *op. cit.*, 1970, p. 50; and also id., *op. cit.*, 1972, p. 19.

This shows us that quantity and quality do not coincide: England assumed (especially with the explosion of the Beatles phenomenon) a cultural leadership (in the sense of offering innovatory cultural contents) and in the field in question it approached the US in terms of economic potential without, however, reaching or surpassing it. The result, as seen by the author, is a curious triangular relationship of the following type:

(The length of vectors approximately represents the flow volume of hits).

The above bears out an observation made by Paul Beaud, who, having studied various sources (ministries, archives, radio/TV) relating to the French music market of the 60's stated: "In examining the material, we arrived at a surprising fact: according to this data, neither the Beatles nor the entire pop culture ever existed[20]. This rather amazing statement may have two possible explanations (which are most probably interrelated and act as common cause):

a) the inadequacy and insufficient reliability of official statistics;

b) the non-correspondence of quality and quantity, in the sense that a message perceived as being radically new and explosive need not necessarily have an equal impact on the quantitative level."

Without wanting to attribute a definite value to the above mentioned observations, but simply wishing to show up an existing problem, it appears necessary, in returning to the subject proper, to strongly underline that the mere collection of quantitative data about the national production of phonograms — even if it should be reliable — will tell us very little about the complex reality of world culture in motion. Already in the 60s an American economist, I. Schiller, strongly underlined that the phenomenon of cultural imperialism had serious economic foundations. Actually it was quite a fad among sociologists to interpret the international spreading of mass culture of United States origin as a phenomenon resulting from the fact that in the United States this culture had originally developed also in response to specific economic exigencies (necessity of an increase in private consumption in contrast to the need of cutting it down during the stage of capitalistic accumulation)[21]. According to a simplified, unilinear interpretation, one tended to argue

---

[20] Cf. Beaud, P., *op. cit.*, p. 68.

[21] Cf. Schiller, H. I., *Mass Communications and American Empire*, Kelley, New York, 1969, p. 112 ff.; for the "culturalistic" interpretation refer to F. Alberoni, *Società, cultura e comunicazioni di massa*, in AA.VV., *Questioni di Sociologia*, 2 vol. La Scuola, Brescia, 1966, vol. II, pp. 487 – 520.

that with the progress of industrialization and modernization also other countries needed such a culture and, therefore, resorted to something previously produced elsewhere, even if some local adjustments were made[22]. This issue is of particular importance and the author has already in the past tried to make a first analysis of the way in which cultural styles are adapted to the countries which import them. For example: The *House of the Rising Sun*, with its painful experience of drugs and emargination, became *Le Pénitencier* in the French translation, a pure and simple prison lament, and similarly, *A Whiter Shade of Pale* with its minute description of the effects of LSD, became *Senza fine* in Italy, describing nothing but the experience of drunkenness. We could give many more examples of the same kind. This interpretation, however, was too "culturalistic" in the sense of giving too much priority to aspects of content and the adaptation of messages produced by the cultural centres to the social characteristics of the peripheries.

In other words, one failed to take account of the enormous economic weight of the cultural industry, especially of the American one, which by the way of the multinationals becomes now directly active in all the dependent countries[23].

In the light of all this it appears necessary to collect data about the production of phonograms, to minutely examine the import/export flows and to identify, by means of qualitative ad-hoc analyses, the cultural content of such flows, even if they are not expressed in the purchase and sale of phonograms but by "imitating" and "adapting" cultural fashions of foreign origin. This is the only way of showing that the production of phonograms is not merely an economic phenomenon but that it forms part of a cultural movement embracing a large part of our world.

Nor should we forget that the multinationals, which frequently decentralize the production away from the places in which the ideas originated add to our difficulties. Yet, difficulties have never been a good reason for denying the existence of problems.

---

[22] Cf. Morin, E., *L'industria culturale*, Il Mulino, Bologna, 1963 (or. ed., *L'esprit du temps*, 1962).

[23] Cf. Del Grosso Destreri, L., *Televisione e stratificazione sociale*, Coop. Libr. Univ., Trento, 1976, chapters I and II.

Documentary Appendix

Elements of Classification of the Demoskopea Sample Inquiry

Geographical zone	N	%
North-west	573	28,8
North-east	379	19,0
Central	385	19,3
South and isles	655	32,9

Size of centre	N	%
Up to 10,000 inhabitants	698	35,0
From 10,000 to 30,000	373	18,7
From 30,000 to 100,000	332	16,7
Over 100,000 inhabitants	589	29,6

Profession of respondent	N	%
Entrepreneurs, free professions, executives	32	1,6
Middle class (upper)	55	2,8
Middle class (middle)	291	14,6
Middle class (lower)	101	5,1
Farmers	88	4,4
Teachers	61	3,4
Students	162	8,1
Workers — middle class	227	11,4
Workers — lower class	132	6,6
Farm labourers	47	2,4
Housewives — upper class	20	1,0
Housewives — middle class	204	10,2
Housewives — lower class	199	10,0
Pensioners and unemployed	373	18,7
Total	1992	100,0

Socio-economic class	N	%
Upper/upper middle	208	10,4
Middle	994	49,9
Lower middle/lower	788	39,6
Total	1992	100,0

Letter from AFI

Dear Professor Del Grosso Destreri,

Referring to your visit and to your letter of April 27, 1979, we now send you the data we have available for a market estimate based on the phonographic material sold in 1977.

Records 45 r.p.m.	17,796,206
Records 33 r.p.m.	16,221,674
Musicassettes	6,562,305
Cartridges	1,185,646
Special records	2,524,828

These figures do not include the records produced for exportation and are taken from a universe composed of 26 out of 34 production companies selected for the purpose.

As to sales in terms of repertoire during the period from 1967 to 1977, we may state, as is indicated in the journal "Musica e Dischi" from October 1978, that they have increased for Italian pop music from 16,000 to 62,500 million and from 10,700 to 5,200 for the same type of foreign music, while classical music has risen from 2,000 to 15,000 million.

As to the manufacture of phonographic products, we believe that since Italy belongs to the countries where the use of "dépot legal" is in force, useful information will be forthcoming from the S.I.A.E., Viale della Letterature, 30 Eur, Rome.

With kind regards,

yours sincerely
The Secretary General

K. Peter Etzkorn

Notes in Defense of Mass Communication Technology

Since music is a performing art, it necessarily depends on interacting individuals and on various types of social relations in order to flourish. Moreover, the complexity of social organizations becomes a basic requirement for performance aspects of musical complexity. Yet it does not follow that social complexity *must* always result in musical complexity; rather, simple types of music frequently exist in rather complex social systems. The obverse, on the contrary, would not seem to be possible. Complex musical systems that require the coordination of different performers and even a high degree of instrumental differentiation are unlikely to be encountered in settings with simple social structures. Musical requirements, as it were, promote social differentiation. The elaboration of social structure as it is connected with the specialization of technological processes parallels the development and manufacture of differentiated musical instruments. To a lesser degree social specialization is required for the separation of instrumental and vocal music, or even for the performance of complex vocal music. Moreover, the more highly elaborated a social structure is, the more likely it will be that social groups use musical manifestations as means to symbolize differences of function and social esteem as markers between and among its constituent social groups. "Religious" music as contrasted with "secular", "serious" as contrasted with "trivial" music are appropriate examples for musical specialities serving as identifiers for social groups, as well as for individual musicians.

In the age of mass media the influence of technology on music has become especially pronounced in activities connected with the diffusion and dissemination of music rather than performance. The propagation of sound which is initially one of the objectives of the refinement of instrument manufacture, has become elaborated through such essentially non-musical technologies as radiowave transmission, or the storing of commands for the preservation of sound on disc and tape. Partly as a result of these technological inventions the potential grew for the further bifurcation of social structure into entire groups of individuals whose involvement with music is primarily of either an active or passive nature. While it must be recognized that this distinction has always obtained, insofar namely as a certain passive tendency could always be found among people attending musical events rather than performing in them. It is mass communications technology, however, that has introduced to the passive recipient of music as additionally qualifying element the fact of physical remoteness from the act of musical performance. Viewed from the perspective of a musical situation, there would appear to be a difference between the individual who is attending a concert, who although sitting passively in the audience, had to actively move self to the location, and the individual who is overhearing as background to another activity the very same, but recorded musical composition. Without doubt, technology cannot be held responsible for having created the category of the uninvolved and remote consumers of music. It is clear that even attenders at concerts are not necessarily involved in the musical event that they are witnessing. While mass technology did not produce the social type of the uninvolved musical consumer, it did create the means for anonymous consumption. It provided the means for musical reproduction even in the privacy of one's personal setting, but most importantly, free from whatever social constraints would be imposed from an individual's presence in an organized public.

Modern mass communications technology, it may be suggested, has created the conditions for differentiating the population into segments of the relatively few musically involved (as creators, producers, and active recipients) and a majority of passive consumers. This categorization would apply equally to all fields of music, from the fields of serious to trivial music. Each field has its "creators" and "consumers". The means of mass communication technology offer the opportunity for the masses to become consumers of finished musical products, uninvolved in the artistic or esthetic process through which the musical works are created. Technology, rather than capitalistic or communistic economic philosophies provide the conditions for separating creators and recipients and hence, for the rise of mass consumerism.

Music like other consumer goods has been used as elements to signify one's claims to social recognition and status, or to symbolize aspects of one's personal identity. The repertory of symbolic devices through which individuals signify their belongingness to a group are many. They range from those rather frequently studied by sociologists, as language usage, speech or leisure patterns to the more subtle gestures practiced by members of groups such as the specific identifications used by members of "secret societies". In simple societies, such as among American Indian tribes, musical performances have been shown, for example, to have served these purposes. Different musical performances helped to identify individual roles within their social environments.

In the age of modern technology, the technological production process is rather undifferentiated between musical types from the recording of a master-tape in a studio setting to the merchandising of the finished product in stores or through mail order. It is the same mass communication industry that manufactures the long-playing record of a Brandenburg Concerto and of an *acid rock* group. Nevertheless social differentiation can be observed. A Bach becomes the acoustic embellishment, say, for the chattering at an elite cocktail reception, while rock music accompanies the social rituals of the younger set. In either setting the respective music is considered appropriate and/or fitting by those in attendance. We find that mass produced music is also being employed along with other mass consumer goods as means of membership identification by subgroups in the population. It is therefore not surprising that musical activities are on the whole not differentiated or analyzed further in their treatment by their audiences. Consumers do not tend to ask questions about the history or esthetics of the apparel that they wear, details of the history of manufacturing process of the automobiles which they drive, or even the philosophical and epistomological assumptions that undergird the semantics of their everyday linguistic usage. The fate of music and its treatment by consumers is not that much different from that of other consumption goods and items in the normal cultural repertoire.

The problem with mass media technology is that the conditions have become maximized by which social involvement in the musical arts become minimized. The mass media offer means for individuals to withdraw into anonymous consumerism. Yet these very technological processes offer an equal potential for greater self-involvement, for more extensive if not necessarily intensive involvement in a wide range of cultural experiences, along with the sharing of cultural goods across historic social boundaries. The means of mass communication technology are making it possible that boundaries between the people and among subgroups be overcome. The very same means, it must also be remembered, have also been used to block out individuals from viewing cultural manifestations of "undesirable" others or of regarding them as desirable. Political control of mass communication technology has given samples of its power as a medium of indoctrination. Here, however, the evil does again not lie within the means of technology, but with the purposes to which the media are used.

Because of the positive potential of mass communication technology for bringing musical manifestations from around the world into even

remote communities, of challenging individuals to become active participants in musical experiences through such processes as studying the
scores, and performing on exotic instruments for enriching one's own
national musical heritage with the artistic expressions of those of other
traditions, observers of contemporary musical life have frequently become
disenchanted with the uncritical acceptance of the status quo in many
quarters. Two observations might be offered at this point. In spite of this
limited use of the available technology for increasing and deepening
musical involvement, there probably has never been a generation that has
experienced as much confrontation with "foreign" musical idioms and
exposure to as much musical change and challenge as the current
generation of the earth's population. Musical experiences all over this
world are in rapid flux in all genres from serious to popular or trivial
music. Second, in spite of a quantitatively very large proportion of the
audience which is musically unsophisticated and largely oriented to
passive consumerism, the impact of education on creating a more
musically critical public cannot be denied. Democratization of the arts,
sharing of artistic experiences outside the circle of privilege and the elites
have become a fact of modern life. In comparison with the golden ages of
medieval Europe, a far larger share of all segments of European (or
Western) society today can be considered musically involved. Finally, the
very advances of musicological scholarship which undergird some of the
esthetic criticisms of this age of mass consumerism owe their refinements
to the accomplishments of mass communication technology.

With the experience of the United States in mind, we will now examine a
number of areas in which phonograph recordings can be shown to have
had a major impact on cultural and scholarly life.

The field of *print publication* has developed entire areas of specialized
publications for the description and analysis of the variety of products of
the sound recording industry. There are commercially oriented but also
more directly scholarly publications that focus on explicit references to
available phonograph recordings that report on musical as well as
technical aspects of high fidelity recordings and equipment, and that in
their own turn have brought into being scholarly discussions of their own
roles within modern society. An example of this particular type of inquiry
would be the examination of the question whether the various sub-types of
the mainstream popular music field are creations of the print media (i.e.
the result of verbal classifications) or genuine musical sub-divisions. In the
light of rather minimal musical differences between, say, rock music and
disco music, the suspicion is tenable that these differences are more the
creations of merchandizers who use print media than indices of the music
per se. Naturally this type of curiosity can be satisfied through empirical
research. While there is not an extensive array, several studies by

the Institute of Ethnomusicology at University of California Los Angeles examining the correlation between merchandizers' terminology about the music of the Beatles and the music itself confirm that there is basis for the suspicion. Mantle Hood found that the general slowing down of the beat in the music could hardly be compared with the comparisons to sexual orgasm metaphorically alleged by writers. In Appendix A I am providing a sample of journals currently available in the USA which contain reviews of phonograph records and equipment while Appendix B offers specialized bibliographic sources that provide easier access to the treasure of recorded sound held in archives by giving discographic details.

Classification of the total output of the recording industry into subcategories usable for musicological scholarship would, of course, be a mammoth undertaking in view of the approximately half billion annual unit production in recent years. This figure is a composite of new material, the republication of old materials, and of musical material produced outside the United States. The production figure of new material in the United States alone may be inferred from the number of annual copyright registrations which has fluctuated around 10,000 (1976: 10,392; 1977: 11,120). While not all copyrighted material is necessarily recorded – an earlier study estimated that less than half was commercially released on phonograph disks – estimates of the contribution of new compositions to the total output can be made. Such estimates would need to consider the average unit production of commercial records, the impact of "hits" with their disproportionate unit production runs, and the number of "cover" recordings. Another source for such information would be performance rights organizations (ASCAP, BMI, SESAC) which keep track of records released from copyrighted composition of their members.

For a recent year (1973) *Billboard* reported a total sale of 484.8 million units for a dollar value of 2.017 billion. Forty-three percent of these were in the form of LP records, with an average of between 10 and 12 tunes per record. Forty percent were in the form of single records, fifteen percent as 8-track cartridges, and two percent as cassettes. Reel to reel and quadrasonic recordings amounted to less than four-tenths of one percent combined. The repertoire of these recordings was classified by *Billboard* as follows:

	%
Popular	65.6
Soul	14.6
Country	10.5
Classical	6.1
Jazz	1.3
All others	1.9

These broad classifications are further refined by merchandizers, radio announcers, and popular writers. Mass marketing stores use a variety of categories for record display racks that refer to performing artists, to style, to period, to lyric content, and any number of other themes. In an earlier paper we reported on how the Philadelphia record group classified hit records from the extended time period from 1940 through 1974. For the purposes of this analysis it was necessary to listen to the sound recordings of all the 540 tunes that had reached the number one position on regularly published popularity charts during that period. These recordings were auditioned (independently by several researchers) and classified by *song type*, *artist type* and *lyric content*. Song type is a classification describing the overall "sound" of the rendition. Song type deals with audible compositional structure, musical arrangement, and vocal interpretation. Ten categories were identified that were grouped into "mainstream" consisting of: rock upbeat, pop upbeat, pop ballad; and "substream" consisting of: folk, country and western, rhythm and blues, jazz, comedy/novelty, and seasonal music. The eight *artist type* categories fall into three broader classifications. "Solo" consisting of: female and male vocalist; "Group" consisting of: female and male vocal, mixed duet, and mixed vocal group; and "Orchestra" distinguishing between: big band and small combo. Finally, *lyric content* was established through the use of traditional modes of content analysis of the song's words.

This type of analysis provided a means for classifying these recordings independently of the categories employed by the commercial interests. Having developed such independent analytic categories then permitted the design of correlational studies intended to answer questions such as: Do recording companies differ in the types of recordings that reach number one positions? (In given periods: Yes.) Does artist type differ by record manufacturer? (Artist types differ by manufacturer and epoch). Does lyric content differ by manufacturer and epoch? (There are no significant differences).

Studies of this type will aid in answering qualitative questions about the role of the commercial interests in modern society. Yet they will need to be rounded out by institutional studies of the industry itself by sociological analyses of the nature of decision making within the music business, of the extent to which marketing information is utilized and as to the sources and the types of such data. In this context analyses are mandated of the interconnectedness of the phonograph business, both internally and internationally, with radio and television broadcasting, with equipment manufacture, moving picture production and live performing ensembles and/or star performers.

Questions concerning the financial backing of the phonograph industry should be raised. Studies should explore relationships between sources and amounts of investment, form of ownership and control, by such indices as size of firm, line of product, type of market, and rate of return. Such analyses in turn would need to be connected with studies of the relative significance of staffing patterns in industry. What, for example, are the recruiting patterns of decision-makers within various divisions of the recording industry? Are there differences between the technical, the marketing, and the artistic staffs? And, if so, what are typical career patterns, if any, of trend setters in the industry?

The roles of companies in influencing the access of artistic products to the open market would need to be analyzed. To what extent does the practice of companies of having "exclusive" contracts with performers (and composers) restrict the free flow of artistic creativity? To what extent do political considerations enter into the propagation of music within the nation and across international boundaries? To what extent does formal "endorsement" and censorship become a variable in influencing the popularity of recorded music? (Does governmental prohibition call forth the use of music as a symbol of resistance to official policy?) While governmental influence may be of marginal concern in the artistic decision making of record companies as far as the selection and treatment of certain repertoires is concerned, its impact on both commercial and archival (library) distribution may well be more significant. Legislation has directly affected the various forms of distribution of music via radio and video broadcasting. Licensees of both commercial and non-commercial (educational) broadcast media need to meet governmental requirements protecting the general consumer. Self-regulations of the industry in the area of preventing material of questionable "taste" to be aired, for example has been a response to these governmental mandates. Legislation also protects economic interests of performing musicians, and composers via copyright rules and basic labor legislation that protects demands of unionized musicians. Sociological study of this broad topic is long overdue. Such study might well produce paradoxical findings such as that the intent of the legislation to promote and sustain artistic pluralism (via insisting on competition between ASCAP, BMI, and SESAC) may be contradicted by other rules that support industry concentration (such as by-products of copyright and labour legislation).

Finally, an area open to statistical analysis should be mentioned. This concerns the study of the holdings and uses of phonograph archives and record libraries. Archiving of recorded sound, of course, offers one of the great opportunities for musical enrichment directly derivative from the invention of the phonograph. As already mentioned before, without these tools musicological scholarship, as we know it today, could not even be dreamed of. In addition, repositories of phonograph records exist on a tremendous scale outside of scholarly archives. Individuals "collect" records, some even for the enjoyment of collecting collectibles. Others store collections as a result of obtaining records and not discarding them. Sociological study of this phenomenon would provide valuable insight on the role of technology in culture. I have not seen any in-depth studies of the phenomenon of record collecting, nor of the holdings and uses of such collections even in music education. And, with the exception of the discographic studies mentioned earlier, there do not appear to be broadly-based sociological studies of the make-up and uses of the enormous record collections in public and university libraries across the United States. Study of both what is collected in the collections, and of who uses what, would appear to be relatively easy to conduct. Such studies would then be coupled with analyses of the make-up and use of private collections. In combination, then, such studies would enable researchers to begin documenting the impact of recorded sound on creating the acoustic environment of society after the invention of the phonograph.

Research on the impact of the phonograph on the cultural life in the United States has been sporadic. There are the occasional studies on selected facets of music on records, but their accretion — even under the best of circumstances — does not amount to a comprehensive assessment of changes wrought on our culture by the invention of this technology.

Appendix A

U.S. Journals Dealing with Phonograph Recordings

The Absolute Sound – (Box 115, Sea Cliff, NY 11579), Audio *Equipment* Analysis.

American Record Guide – (1 Windsor Pl., Melville, NY 11746), Record Review Monthly.

Audio (North Am. Publishing Co., 401 N. Broad Street, Philadelphia, PA), Record Reviews.

Audio Critic (Box 392, Bronxville, NY 10708), Audio *Equipment* Reviews.

Billboard (9000 Sunset Blvd., Los Angeles, CA 90069), Weekly Trade Paper.

Down Beat (222 W. Adams Street, Chicago, IL 60606). Bi-weekly, Devoted to Jazz and Blues.

Ethnomusicology (University of Michigan, Ann Arbor, MI), Record Reviews, Articles.

Film Music Notebook (Box 25198, West Los Angeles, CA 90025), News and Interviews.

High Fidelity (Great Barrington, MA 01230), Record and Equipment Reviews.

Journal of Jazz Studies (c/o Transaction Inc., Rutgers University, New Brunswick, NY 08903), Bi-annual Collection of Essays.

Miklos Rozsa Society Newsletter (319 Avenue C, No. 11-H, New York, NY 10009), Up-to-date News on Film Music.

Modern Recording (Cowan Publishing Co., 14 Vanderventer Ave., Port Washington, NY 11050), For the Home Recordist and Classical Reviews.

Musical America (Publishing House, Great Barrington, MA 01230), Covers Entire Spectrum of Educated Music-Going.

The Musical Quarterly (866-3rd Ave., New York, NY 10022), Record Reviews.

Music Educators Journal (1902 Association Drive, Center for Educational Associations, Reston, VA 22091), Glossy Magazine on all Aspects of Music.

Record World (1700 Broadway, New York, NY 10019), The East Coast Billboard.

Rolling Stone (625-3rd Street, San Francisco, CA), More Than Half of Content is Devoted to Music.

Stereo Review (1 Park Ave., New York, NY 10016), Monthly Review of Records; Includes Section on Popular Music.

Appendix B

Bibliographic Sources of Scholarly Works Dealing with Phonograph Recordings

Allen, Walter C., Studies in Jazz Discography, New Brunswick, N. J. Institute of Jazz Studies, Rutgers University, 1971.

Association for Recorded Sound Collections. A preliminary directory of sound recordings collections in the United States and Canada. Prepared by a committee of the Association for Recorded Sound Collections, N.Y., N.Y. Public Library, 1967, 157p. (Collections alphabetically by state; brief information as to content of collections; many private collections included).

Brieglieb, Ann, ed., Directory of Ethnomusicological Sound Recording Collections in the U.S. and Canada, Ann Arbor, MI, SEM, 1971, 46p. (Special Series #2).

Currall, Henry F. J., Phonograph record libraries, their organization and practice. London, Crosby Lockwood and Son, 1970, 303p. (A manual for the administration of a record library).

Dimmick, Mary L., The Rolling Stones: An annotated bibliography, Pittsburgh, PA, University of Pittsburgh Graduate School of Library and Information Sciences, 1972.

Discography Series. (Discographies of some of the major song composers of the romantic period). Nos. 1 – 4, J. F. Weber, ed., pp. 5 – 7, Peter Morse, ed. N.Y. 1970.

Merriam, Alan P., African Music on L.P., An annotated discography, Evanston, Illinois, Northwestern University Press, 1970, 200p.

New form of musical scholarships, i.e. Myers, Kurtz, and Richard S. Hill, Record ratings, the Music Library's Association's index of record reviews, N.Y., Crown Publishers, 1956, 440p. (ML156.9 M992R – Wash. U.).

UNESCO, Discographies on Oriental Music, Paris, 1952, Collection Phonothèque National (Paris) 4,569 discs, Musé de l'Homme (Paris) 1,007 recordings, Regensburg collection of European Folk Music.

U.S. Library of Congress. Music Division, Recording Laboratory, Folk Music: A catalog of folk songs, ballads, dances, instrumental pieces, and folk tales of the United States and Latin America on phonograph records, Washington, D.C. Library of Congress, 1964, 107p. (Earlier listings 1948, 1953, and 1959).

Mária Sági

Music on Records in Hungary

In 1975 Elöd Juhász (in his "Around Our Records": *Kritika*, 1975, no. 3, p. 24) describes Hungarian record production as rather backward although, in spite of all shortcomings, record turnover in Hungary had trebled during the preceding years, and the share of artistic records had also grown. What he particularly condemns is the long production time (one year) which is largely due to the fact that the moulds are manufactured in Sweden, and the distance makes corrections difficult. He quotes the following data for the growth of the number of artistic records: 6.4 per cent in 1965, 6.8 per cent in 1968, more than 30 per cent in 1974 and 40 to 42 per cent in 1975 (for comparison, the corresponding figures are about 10 per cent in the United States and some 30 per cent in France and the FRG). Examples of the export of Hungarian records are as follows: 47,000 in 1973, 55,000 in 1974 (80 per cent "serious music") to the United States, our largest capitalist market. Juhász also states that the Record Manufacturing Enterprise, in spite of the shortcomings, is a profitable undertaken even without state subsidy.

The new galvanographic factory at Dorog which has been built up since then, has increased the previous manufacturing capacity by about 2.5 million pieces. The relevant statistical data are as in the table on next page.

As can be seen, 2.5 million more records were manufactured in 1977 than in 1976. At present, i.e. in 1979, the number of records produced and sold is an annual 7.5 million which is about three times the number of ten years ago (1968 – 1978).

The qualitative development of the records manufactured is character-ized by a substantial growth of the share of stereophonic records: it was 20 per cent of all records in 1970 (59 per cent of records with serious music) and 77 per cent in 1975 – 76 (including 96 per cent of serious music records).

Retrospective Data

Identification	1973	1974	1975	1976	1977	In % of previous year
Time of works registered in minutes	4310'36"	4618'47"	4961'10"	4557'29"	4867'13"	106.8
Number of record types	897	950	880	857	955	111.4
Number of records published	2940019	3064785	3411107	3842570	6291672	163.7
Number of records marketed in Hungary	2871482	2990293	3295538	3867570	5661778	146.4
Number of records marketed abroad	740499	664076	960915	898209	1153380	128.4
Total	3611981	3654369	4256453	4765779	6815158	143.0

Production of Records According to Genres

All records in Hungary are produced by the Hungarian Record Manufacturing Enterprise but are marketed under three different names:

Hungaroton — for serious music, original folklore, literature
Qualiton   — for operettas, gypsy music
Pepita   — other music.

At present, 20 per cent of the records contain serious music, 4 — 5 per cent literature or documents and the rest entertainment music. The number of new editions per year is:

> 70 serious music
> 35 entertainment music
> 25 literature or documents.

In the past decade not only the number of records marketed has risen but a shift has been observed in favour of serious music. Here are the relevant data published in the Statistical Bulletin:

	1973	1974	1975	1976	1977
	As percentage of all records published				
Serious music	17.7	24.9	28.8	32.6	22.1
Entertainment music, like dance, operetta and art songs	74.4	70.0	67.2	61.7	71.2
Folklore	2.2	2.2	1.5	1.0	1.5
Labour movement songs	0.3	1.3	0.8	1.0	1.2
Prose	5.4	1.4	1.7	3.7	4.1
Other	—	0.2	—	—	—
Total	100.0	100.0	100.0	100.0	100.0
	As percentage of all records sold				
Serious music	20.1	26.7	29.8	29.2	21.2
Entertainment music inclusive dance, operetta and art songs	72.9	67.2	64.8	65.5	71.8
dance music therein	60.9	58.1	54.1	52.3	—
Folk music, labour movement songs, prose	7.0	6.1	5.4	5.3	7.0
Total	100.0	100.0	100.0	100.0	100.0

As our data shows, the share of serious music increased till 1976 in both publishing and marketing and fell down to 22 — 21 per cent in 1977, a figure characteristic also of the present day. Entertainment music showed an opposite trend by its decreasing share in marketing.

As a little detour let me say a few words about our publication policy concerning serious music. Essentially four trends can be distinguished:

1. The first trend consists in publishing the entire oeuvre of the greatest Hungarian composers (like Liszt, Bartók). A ten-year programme came to an end in 1978, when Bartók's works were published on 38 records. Nevertheless works by Bartók continue to appear in the interpretation of young artists reflecting the artistic life of the country. The publication of the entire oeuvre of Liszt and that of Kodály has been started. The series include works never published before, like Liszt's *Legend of St. Elisabeth* or the *Christ Oratorio*.

2. The second trend consists in publishing works of European value having some relation to Hungary. These include, for instance, Haydn's complete repertoire (on account of his Hungarian patron Esterházy), works of minor masters (chiefly Austrians) whose manuscripts were found in Hungary. Each edition heavily relies on Hungarian musicological research.

3. The third trend consists in publishing the repertoire of the best Hungarian performing artists (for instance, Beethoven's Ninth Symphony conducted by János Ferencsik).

4. The fourth trend consists in the publication of music composed by contemporary Hungarian artists.

The largest firms in the world cannot boast of better results than those achieved in Hungary. Our country has even earned a UNESCO prize.

The highest number of records with serious music — about 50,000 — was published in 1978.

Within entertainment music, 90 per cent of the records are for juvenile consumers (rock, beat, pop, country music). Favourite records in this genre are sold in 50,000 to 100,000 copies. The peak has so far been somewhere above 150,000.

A few socio-musicological comments may be added on the basis of the turnover of serious music records sold in Hungary. In their papers published in the monthly *Muzsika*, Jenö Bors and Mária Feuer analyse public taste on the basis of the "hit records" of the past ten years.

The table below may be of interest to foreign readers. It is a list of serious music records giving the numbers sold between 1964 and 1973:

	Copies sold
Bach: Toccata and Fugue in D Minor	47,713
Vivaldi: Four Seasons	over 26,000
Beethoven: Fifth Symphony	over 26,000

	Copies sold
Kodály: Háry János Suite	over 26,000
Bartók: Music for Strings, Percussion and Celesta	12,695
Puccini: Madame Butterfly [excerpts]	12,257
Erkel: László Hunyadi (opera)	12,178
Kodály: Budavár Te Deum, oratorio	
Bartók: Concerto	about 11,000
Bartók: Count Bluebeard's Castle [recorded in 1963]	
Liszt: Christ Oratorio	
Kodály: Psalmus Hungaricus	about 9,000

Retail Prices of Records

The prices of stereo and mono records have, since April 1, 1969, been identical. Differences only occurred according to size and genre.

In 1970, the price of an entertainment record of 30 cm was 66. — Ft, that of records with serious music being 60. — Ft. In all other sizes serious music has remained unchanged or has slightly risen. The table below shows an exact picture of the changes:

In 1970	Entertainment Ft	Art Ft
SLPX-LPX, 30 cm	66. —	60. —
SLP-LP, 25 cm	50. —	45. —
EP, 17 cm	28. —	26. —
SP, 17 cm	22. —	20. —
SPS Licence, 17 cm	44. —	
SP (60,000 — 80,000)		15. —
SHLX (inexpensive series)		30. —

(As from 1970, the price of some pop records has risen to 70. — Ft, as e.g. the Omega records.)

In 1975	Entertainment Ft	Art Ft
30 cm records	66. —	60. —
	70. —	
	80. —	
	85. —	

In 1975	Entertainment Ft	Art Ft
30 cm licences	150. –	150. –
25 cm	50. –	45. –
17 cm SP	36. –	20. –
	22. –	
17 cm licences	40. –	
SHLX (inexpensive series)		35. –
Cassette (as from 1976)	150. –	120. –

In 1978	Entertainment Ft	Art Ft
30 cm record	90. –	70. –
Same (Special series)		50. –
Same (licences)	150. –	150. –
25 cm	50. –	50. –
17 cm	30. –	30. –
		20. –
17 cm (licences)	40. –	
Cassette	150. –	120. –
Cassette (Special series)		100. –

Export and Import

The number of imported records has shown a substantial growth since 1970. In 1976 six times as many records were imported as in 1970 (1,422,300 as against 233,800) which corresponds to 3.5 times the 1972 imports.

The Statistical Bulletin gives a detailed account of the records marketed in 1977.

About 30 per cent of our records go to foreign countries, but in addition we also sell master tapes. Besides the socialist countries, our best partners are France, Great Britain, the USA, the FRG, Japan, Spain. Our export to capitalist countries consists exclusively of serious music.

Tapes and Cassettes

Recent years have witnessed the appearance of programme cassettes in addition to the tapes.

In 1976, the turnover in programme cassettes was 97,000, including two-thirds of home-produced recordings with serious and entertainment

Number of Records Sold

	In Hungary				Abroad			
	30 cm	Other (mostly 17 cm)	Total	In % of previous year	30 cm	Other (mostly 17 cm)	Total	In % of previous year
Made in Hungary								
Serious music	754753	20671	775424	110.6	452433	–	452433	106.8
Entertainment music	2034478	1529957	3564435	164.0	651365	415	651780	141.8
Folk music	80647	6513	87160	187.2	26495	402	26897	182.1
Labour movement music	26546	51421	77967		–	–	–	
Prose	181962	53021	234983		–	–	–	
Other	–	1224	1224		–	–	–	
Total	3078386	1662807	4741193	153.5	1130293	817	1131110	125.9
Imported								
Serious music	164295	–	164295	62.0	–	–	–	–
Entertainment music	461706	21294	483000	98.6	–	–	–	–
Folk music	27950	640	28590		–	–	–	–
Labour movement music	–	–	–	132.6	–	–	–	–
Prose	3963	–	3963		–	–	–	–
Other	–	–	–		–	–	–	–
Total	657914	21934	679848	187.2	–	–	–	–

Number of Records Sold. Made in Hungary and Imported

	In Hungary				Abroad			
	30 cm	Other (mostly 17 cm)	Total	In % of previous year	30 cm	Other (mostly 17 cm)	Total	In % of previous year
Serious music	919048	20671	939719	97.3	452433	–	452433	106.8
Entertaining music	2496184	1551251	4047435	152.0	651365	415	651780	141.8
Folk music	108597	7153	115750		26495	402	26897	
Labour movement music	26546	51421	77967	181.6	–	–	–	182.1
Prose	185925	53021	238946		–	–	–	
Other	–	1224	1224		–	–	–	
Grand total	3736300	1684741	5421041	140.2	1130293	817	1131110	125.9

Number of Tapes and Cassettes Sold with Programmes

	For domestic use				For export			
	Home production	Import	Total	In % of previous year	Home production	Import	Total	In % of previous year
Serious music	39420	−32	39388	246.3	12866	—	12866	—
Entertainment music	165576	21952	187528	234.6	8058	—	8058	—
Folk music	1586	62	1648	—	1346	—	1346	—
Labour movement songs	637	—	637	1386.3	—	—	—	—
Prose	11536	—	11536	—	—	—	—	—
Other	—	—	—	—	—	—	—	—
Total	218755	21982	240737	248.4	22270	—	22270	—

	Total			
	Home production	Import	Total	In % of previous year
Serious music	52286	−32	52254	—
Entertainment music	173634	21952	195586	—
Folk music	2932	62	2994	—
Labour movement songs	637	—	637	—
Prose	11536	—	11536	—
Other	—	—	—	—
Total	241025	21982	263007	—

Total of Records and Programmed Tapes Sold

For domestic use

	Home production	Import	Total	In % of previous year
Records	4741193	679848	5421041	140.2
Programme tapes	218755	21982	240737	248.4
Total	4959948	701830	5661778	146.4

For export

	Home production	Import	Total	In % of previous year
Records	1131110	–	1131110	125.9
Programme tapes	22270	–	22270	–
Total	1153380	–	1153380	–

Total

	Home production	Import	Total	In % of previous year
Records	5872303	679848	6552151	137.5
Programme tapes	241025	21982	263007	–
Total	6113328	701830	6815158	–

music. According to the Statistical Bulletin, 2.5 times more programme tapes were sold in 1977 than in 1976. The details are given in Tables on page 119.

The total turnover of tapes and cassettes in 1977 can be seen from the table on page 120 revealing that the turnover of records had grown by 40 per cent and that of programmed cassettes by 148.4 per cent.

Number of Record Players and Tape Recorders in Households

The number of record players sold in 1975 was 86,500 and in 1976, 83,400. On analyzing the data from earlier years, a slow rise can be registered as from 1962 (when their number was 30,600), after which it suddenly soared to the 1975 level.

The purchase of tape recorders shows a different tendency: in 1970 there was a very sudden rise (from 6300) to 79,300 and from this year on a gradual increase can be observed up to the 95,100 pieces in 1976.

Turnover of Record Players and Tape Recorders

Year	Record players sold		Tape recorders sold		Average price (forints)	
	1000 pieces	Million forints	1000 pieces	Million forints	Record players	Tape recorders
1962	12.0	17	10.5	–	1 417	–
1965	27.3	28	6.3	24	1 011	3 825
1970	28.8	52	79.3	268	1 799	3 381
1971	31.5	56	88.0	293	1 762	3 334
1972	30.6	58	71.9	251	1 895	3 491
1973	41.4	79	83.8	257	1 908	3 067
1974	68.0	131	88.8	273	1 926	3 074
1975	86.5	173	92.5	295	2 000	3 189
1976	83.4	166	95.1	317	1 990	3 333

These figures should presumably be completed with the number of record players and tape recorders imported via tourism.

To conclude, let me mention that our survey — thanks to the courtesy of the Hungarian Record Producing Enterprise — contains also previously unpublished data.

Bibliography

Bors, Jenö, Jön az uj közönség (The new public is coming), *Muzsika*, 1974, No. 3, p. 1−2.

Breuer, János, Fények és árnyékok hanglemezgyártásunkban (Light and shadow in our record production), *Muzsika*, 1973, No. 10, p. 1 – 3.

Feuer, Mária, Igények és lehetöségek (Demands and facilities), *Muzsika*, 1974, No. 4, p. 39 – 41.

–, Bestseller lemezek (Best seller records), *Muzsika*, 1974, No. 5, p. 30 – 31.

Hungaroton évkönyv 1978. (Hungaroton Annual).

Juhász, Elöd, Hanglemezeink háza-táján (Around our sound records), *Kritika*, 1975, No. 3, p. 24.

Komlós, Katalin, Komolyzenei hanglemez ismertetések (Description of records with serious music), *Muzsika*, 1975, No. 1 – 12.

–, Komolyzenei hanglemez ismertetések (Description of records with serious music), *Muzsika*, 1976, No. 1 – 12.

–, Komolyzenei hanglemez ismertetések (Description of records with serious music), *Muzsika*, 1977, No. 1 – 12.

Közmüvelödés 1972 – 76. Bp. 1978. Központi Statisztikai Hivatal (p. 146) (Public culture 1972 – 1976).

Statisztikai Tájékoztató. Közmüvelödés 1977. (Statistical Bulletin. Public Culture 1977) Bp. 1978. Egyetemi Számitóközpont (p. 207).

Grigory L. Golovinsky

On Some Music-Sociological Aspects of the Phonogram. The Record in Soviet Musical Culture

In the first part of my paper I should like to deal with some problems inherent in the development of the technical means of our civilization. In the second part I will briefly report about the activities of "Melodia", the major record producing firm in our country.

1. The musical culture of our time is exposed to the gigantic and as yet not fully realized impact of the mass media (radio, television, sound recording, film). Under this impact changes have occurred in the status of music in society, in its forms of existence and in the ways in which it is consumed. It suffices to picture modern and particularly young persons and their extensive contact with music which accompanies them during their working hours, in shops or cafés, at the cinema or theatre, and of course at home, to realize even from these extrinsic features the striking difference between our epoch and previous development eras of musical culture.

Another feature of our era is the marked increase in non-concert forms of music consumption. The sublime act of "music listening" in its traditional, classical conception so dear to the heart of the professional musician, is linked with the highest possible degree of absorption in the world of sounds, with the highest possible degree of detachment from everyday life (which is ideally promoted by the atmosphere of a concert hall or music theatre). This act has retained and obviously will retain its great importance as the aesthetically perfect form of perception.

But today, this form of listening is far from being the dominating one. On the contrary, it is in quantity clearly lagging behind the other forms of perception that might be defined as "accompanying" and "synthetic". The first one signifies the consumption of music as background to other activities – at work or at home – which command most of one's attention; in these cases music is often heard indiscriminately, the listener being quite unaware of who has composed it and of what he actually hears (a typical case in point is the radio set switched on throughout the day and tuned in on a music and information programme – in our country a programme called "Mayak" (Radio Beacon)).

Synthetic indicates that music is absorbed in connection with a series of pictures or words that is in the foreground. Here again the extent and variety of these connections are without counterpart in earlier epochs. People perceive music when watching a feature film or an animated film, when turning on their favourite radio or television programme and hearing the signation tune, and also when watching figure skating or gymnastics in the stadium or on television. One may say that this type of perception often implies that people hear music without being aware of it.

Let me illustrate this thought with the following example. Here in Vienna, I saw the movie "Apocalypse now" by Francis Coppola, which was a box-office hit. One of the most impressing scenes in this movie is the attack of a helicopter armada opening massed fire; the musical accompaniment chosen to this scene is Wagner's "Ride of the Valkyries". One can easily imagine that some people, and especially young people, may hear for the first time this marvellous musical fragment not in a concert but in the movie. And it may well be that they will not be aware of having listened to music by Wagner. Moreover, this musical fragment may in their imagination have a pugnaceous-aggressive and triumphant-intoxicating character, because of the association with the mentioned scene. The musical configuration created by Wagner, however, is much richer and more varied, the expression of strength is not aggressive and the enthusiastic ecstasy is not caused by a sensation of triumph but rather by the sensation of free flight. The distortion of the contents of serious music by putting it to use in the synthetic arts is a widespread and very specific phenomenon that goes beyond the scope of this paper.

From the above one may draw the following conclusion: our epoch is characterized by an unprecedented increase in the share of music in people's lives and by the penetration of music into the most diverse spheres of social activity (not alone of art). These well-known circumstances have a number of important implications both for society and for the human personality as well as for the art of music itself.

For this reason we are especially pleased that a renowned international organization like MEDIACULT, which coordinates and pools the efforts of researchers from various countries, has decided to focus its attention in the oncoming decade on the sphere of musical communication. Among the many aspects to be researched, I attribute particular importance to the "Role of the Technical Media in Cultural Communication", as put forth in Kurt Blaukopf's paper, published in "Mediacult Newsletter" No. 24. In the following we shall try and take up some of the issues.

A. The appearance of a specialized industry providing for high-quality transmission and reception of musical sounds across a distance as well as for their recording and reproduction. Like every technology it has an inherent trend towards continuous refinement which opens up new possibilities to the creators and the consumers of art. One result is the huge and constantly expanding market for home equipment and the impact of this equipment on musical perception (example: music recorded on disc has to comply with standards different from music played in the concert hall). The rapid spreading of technical equipment for home recording and reproduction as an integral part of modern civilization which is far ahead of the dissemination and appropriation of cultural values, exerts a complex, contradictory and still unexplored influence on the cultures of the different regions on our planet (example: transistors used by the most remote tribes of the far North, et al.).

B. The predominant form of music consumption in our modern society, which no longer takes place in the concert hall but primarily in the home, gives rise to a special complex of diverse, often contradictory trends. On the one hand, it holds the possibility of sharing in the treasures accumulated throughout human history, the possibility of striking a balance between the artistic-musical cognizance of people living in big cultural centres and those living on the remote periphery (which is of particular importance in a vast country like ours).

On the other hand, it has already been pointed out by great musicians and researchers that the extraordinary ease of access to and the everyday character of the contact with art music holds an enormous danger. A passive kind of perception is gaining ground, a neutral, indiscriminate attitude towards musical sounds, which through systematic and pro-longed contact with music dulls the acuteness and intensity of artistic-musical perception (sometimes causing it to atrophy) and threatens to degrade music to the level of a common, everyday sound background.

Equally important is the socio-psychological aspect. On the one hand, music has entered the home as an indispensable accompaniment to our lives, as emotional, almost empathic resonator, or simply as a voice or symbol representing another human being. And this is of paramount importance to modern man with his difficulty of establishing personal contacts, in particular to people living alone whose number is growing all over the world.

On the other hand, music sounding from the radio or a phonogram deprives the listener of the immediate contact with the performing musician, a contact that is of more than mere artistic significance. The listener does no longer feel to be part of a collective (even a very small one) that is created by the reproduction and perception of a musical work, because he loses the contact with the musicians and with the other listeners (let us recall that the establishment of artistic-psychological contacts among people has forever been part of the art of music). Already W. Furtwängler wrote about music as a joint experience that is missed by the radio listener. This lack of contact which is (often unconsciously) felt by the modern listener, rouses the need for compensation. Hence the heightened interest observed in our country (and probably also in other countries) in the personalities of those creating the music, the wish to meet them and to hear their opinions on musical (and non-musical!) issues. In our country this demand has generated diverse information formats: television and radio magazines and "clubs for interesting encounters", where the author of the music to be performed converses with his listeners; radio and television interviews with composers and performers, which very often go beyond the purely musical scope. I believe that this desire also accounts for the success of certain television films that give insight into the process of musical creation taking place in front of our eyes (apart from the best Karajan-films, I refer to Soviet examples like "The Sixth Symphony of Tchaikovski" with the conductor J. Temirkanov and the films with the conductor E. Mravinski). To me the most interesting element in these films are not the hands but the face of the person re-creating the music; because it is the face of the conductor that displays most completely his intellectual world and his personality.

2. Sound recording is one of the most important modern techniques of storing and disseminating musical art. The development and widespread use of sound recording has engendered a multitude of problems of a technical, socio-musical, socio-psychological and purely aesthetic order. Many of them are treated at this seminar. We may say that in the many-facetted sphere of interaction between music and society very few facets have been left untouched by sound recording. Let me single out just a few of them.

It was sound recording that opened up a wide range of ways in which to use music for diverse social purposes of both artistic and non-artistic nature: the range extends from music at the place of work, via music in medicine, in foreign-language studies, to the musical accompaniment of callisthenics, figure skating and to musical interval signals of broadcasting stations. I have already referred to the diverse implications of this use.

It was sound recording that added one more gem to the artistic treasury of mankind by making it possible to capture one more manifestation of human genius, namely the art of interpretation, which in former times disappeared without trace. Our descendants will not only be able to read the novels of Faulkner and Hemingway, to listen to the symphonies of Shostakovitch and Hindemith, to watch the paintings of Picasso and Rehrich, but they will also get an impression of our epoch through interpretations by conductors like Furtwängler and Casals, Shalyapin and Richter. In brackets I would like to add that since the advent of sound recording the science and art of interpretation have been given a firm material basis.

Let me further observe that thanks to sound recording, to the disc and the cassette, the creative artist, the composer, has been given the previously unknown possibility of getting into contact with his listener. Not with a hypothetical listener who may not exist at all, as it happens in the case of music broadcasts, buth with *his* listener who is interested in and needs a particular work. As an instrument for the mass-dissemination of compositional works, especially of contemporary music, the role of sound recording is only comparable to the introduction of music printing, which it surpasses, however, by the ease in which anyone can gain a musical impression. I shall refer back to this issue later on.

A special aspect of the problem in question is the purchase of musical sound recordings for personal use and individual forms of consumption. It may seem that we are concerned with a purely economic process, but when taking a closer look we realize that it is just another music-sociological phenomenon, which, moreover, is highly typical of our era.

The act of buying a record (cassette) demonstrates above all a conscious choice, evincing an *active* attitude towards the musical phenomenon, the genre, the type of music in question or towards the performing artist or the performing collective.

Incidentally, it should be mentioned that the findings of empirical, sociological research demonstrate how in light, entertainment music the performer grows in the eyes of the listener, almost fully representing of the music performed: the common listener finds it easier to name the popular record or the singer (the band) than the author of the work. The active attitude differentiates the buyer and consumer of a record from the radio and TV-listener, who is very often characterized by a passive, neutral attitude towards the transmitted music.

Let us also take note of the fact that in the above case a specific, relatively small part is selected from the entire, almost infinite ocean of music offered through the various mass media channels, and becomes an object of personal use. We are concerned with a peculiar phenomenon of very specific kinds and types of music being appropriated to form a personal sonic continuum subordinate to the owner. It is almost impossible to exaggerate the implications of this appropriation.

Contrary to some other works of art, a work of music has always been an "object of repeated use". Repeated listening to favourite pieces is one of the characteristic forms of the existence of music. In the past repeated listening depended, on the one hand, on the ability to play an instrument and to sing, on the other hand, on the intensity of the concert and theatre life in a given area. These factors substantially restricted the possibility of satisfying individual musical needs. As to the early stages of artistic development and later on in folklore, with popular examples being known to all members of a given community, repeated performance and listening were in principle open to everyone. In this context, however, there were other limitations: the limitations of social life with its many prohibitions and taboos, specific circumstances as the necessary prerequisite for a work to be performed, etc.

All these restrictions and limitations do not apply to the contemporary owner of a disc or tape recording. The absence of social, technical or other factors regulating the frequency of repetition of a work of music permits unlimited (often daily) listening to a favourite recording.

This, however, implies the danger of a severe restriction of the musical horizon which is very often determined by fads and fashions and not by true artistic values. In addition, frequent listening to one given, recorded interpretation generates an aesthetic stereotype and a static orientation towards one single type of music. The inevitable consequence is an impoverishment of the inner world of man. The paradox of the current situation lies in the fact that, although everyone seems perfectly free to construct his own musical world (as pointed out above), people, and especially young people, prove to be unfree, exposed and subject to fashions, publicity and other means of influencing the personality.

The listening frequency has specific implications not only for the consumer but also for the entire musical culture. One must take account of the fact that the mass listener gives his particular attention at any given time to a small number of latest "hits" (popular classics, entertainment hits, recordings of rock groups, etc.). In most cases these are also the items repeatedly played on radio and television. The eventual result is the phenomenon of "hackneyed music": the aesthetic qualities of a work are worn off by excessive repetition and it loses its original impact. Even if individual examples of classical music (e.g., "Eine kleine Nachtmusik" by Mozart or the First Concert by Tchaikovski) that enter the sphere of "mass listening" still retain a certain, though by no means unlimited aesthetic strength, the majority of popular hits, pieces of beat groups etc. lack the strength to resist the strain of multiple and almost daily repetition, they amortize very fast and disappear from the scene. Hence the strong impetus towards renewal, towards the replacement of one fashion by the next, towards the rapid turnover of "stars" that is so characteristic of the musical sphere. The changeability of fashion in the field of light, entertainment music has long been manifest. But under the impact of the media for mass dissemination and reproduction (not only of the phonogram, but also of radio, television and film) it has become enormously accelerated.

I shall now move on to the second part of my paper.

3. In the USSR the sound recording industry is state-owned; as a result record production is practically independent of the market situation and becomes an instrument of the government's cultural policy. The activities of the nationwide Soviet firm "Melodia" (founded in 1964) are oriented towards the planned growth of record production in diverse categories, in order to satisfy the varied needs of the developing musical culture.

This culture is founded on the domestic and the world classics. "Melodia" regularly issues record cycles and individual recordings to ensure the continuous supply of the listener with all that is most valuable in the musical art of the world. One ought to mention such unique editions as the complete works of P. I. Tchaikovski, S. S. Prokofiev and D. D. Shostakovitch, which offer the listener new interpretations of well-known works and acquaint him with pieces never recorded before. The monumental, complete works of Tchaikovski (more than 100 discs), for instance, include his earlier operas "Mandragora", "The Opritchnik", "The Voyevoda", his liturgy and night vespers for choir. The complete works of Shostakovitch include recordings of his opera "The Nose", the Alto Sonata, the 15th Quartet. Under preparation is a cycle called "History of Russian Music on Discs", presenting the best examples of Russian music from the era of Peter I up to our time. The grandiose collection "From the World History of the Art of Interpretation" (about 200 discs) will offer an opportunity to the listener to get acquainted with the best renderings by the greatest conductors, singers and instrumentalists of past and present.

Folklore holds a special position in contemporary musical life. One has come to recognize its high aesthetic value and its strong and fruitful influence on musical creation. In our country we observe a constantly growing interest in folklore, manifesting itself in extensive theoretical and field research into folklore and in the growing number of folk groups and collectives. At the same time, empirical sociological inquiries demonstrate a certain disparity between the musical consciousness of the masses, particularly of the young people living in big towns, and the genuine, authentic folklore aspects of our musical culture (the so-called "mass consciousness" perceives folklore mostly in arrangements for the entertainment stage).

Thus it becomes necessary to introduce the best part of the gigantic resources compiled by the folklore researchers of the country into everyday musical and cultural life. The folklore anthologies already edited by "Melodia" and devoted to the individual peoples of the country are now to be followed by a unique cycle called "The Orally Handed-Down

Musical Traditions of the Peoples of the USSR" (20 discs), which will for the first time in the history of sound recording comprise the folklore of 150 peoples and tribes (the commentaries are planned to be published in Russian and English). In this context I should like to mention another very interesting publication, the series "From the Collection of the Folklore Expert" edited by the publishing house "Sovietski kompositor" (The Soviet Composer) together with "Melodia". Each part of this series comprises a selection of sheet music taken from the field research collections, an essay informing about the customs and ceremonies linked with a certain song and about the folk singers themselves, photographic illustrations and the most interesting sound recordings (on flexible discs). Among the songs published in this series are "Song of the Timber Rafters on the Yenisei", "Northern Lullabies" and "Wedding Songs from Glinka's Home Country" (the researcher pictures the current practice of the traditional folklore which was the source for the great composer).

One important production sector of "Melodia" is devoted to records for the music education of the masses, as well as for didactic-paedagogical purposes. Apart from the manifold popular literature about music addressed to the general reader and edited by our publishing houses, "Melodia" offers recordings of lectures about music, illustrated with sound examples. Among the most outstanding editions of this kind is the cycle "The People's University of Culture" (45 discs) issued together with the Moscow Conservatory. The four parts of this cycle report about the means of musical expression, about genres and forms, as well as about the lives and work of the greatest composers of the 18th to the 20th centuries, from Bach to Shostakovitch and Shtchedrin. The basic principle of popularization is the following: the general features of creation and the biography of the composer are contained in the text of a booklet enclosed with the record. But what is most important and valuable to the listener, namely a lively and vivid presentation of the music, of the works illustrating the composer's style, is recorded on disc (often spoken by the authors themselves who are renowned music teachers) and goes along with the performance of the works themselves.

"Melodia" has released phono-chrestomathies for the music classes of secondary schools and music schools for children, which contain all the sound material required for illustrations in class. Together with the Conservatory and the "Gnessin" Music Academy audio aids for students are edited. One of the most famous teachers from the ranks of the performing artists, for instance, talks about his interpretations of the works of a given composer, which is followed by a recording of his performance.

Of inestimable value to culture are the historical recordings preserving the voices and works of eminent artists of the past. Difficult and laborious restoration work has made it possible to release records with the voices of Tolstoi, Block, Briussov, and Jessenin reading their own works. Of particular interest to musicians is an album with four records entitled "D. D. Shostakovitch speaking" (duration 115 minutes), with speeches given by the great composer, starting with his radio address in the war year 1941.

The album "G. G. Neuhaus in Class" gives an impression of the art of one of the most eminent teachers and pianists. These recordings of lessons made directly in the classroom have captured a complete artistic conception manifesting itself in the work with the students and in the interpretation of Schumann's Symphonic Etudes, Chopin's Ballads and of works by Debussy. Finally, I should like to mention the cycle "The Art of F. I. Shaliapin", which contains a collection of all the recordings made with the great singer.

In conclusion a few words on consumer interests. There is a stable demand for recordings of domestic classics, especially for works by Tchaikovski and Rakhmaninov. Among foreign composers, baroque composers (especially Bach and Vivaldi) and Mozart (316,000 copies of a recording of his G-minor Symphony have been distributed within 5 – 6 years) are particularly popular. There is considerable interest in the Soviet classics (19,000 copies of the recording of Shostakovitch's opera "The Nose" were sold within a very short period of time, more precisely since 1976), and in the works by the masters of the middle generation, such as Shtchedrin (32,000 copies of the ballet music to "Anna Karenina" have been sold since 1973), Boris Tchaikovski, Tishtchenko, and many others.

Let me briefly summarize what has been said. The mass media, and in particular sound recording, open up indeterminable possibilities in diverse spheres. Among others the gigantic possibility of mass access to the treasures of musical culture. At the same time the impact of the mass media on society, just like the impact of any technical innovation on civilization, is contradictory and will also engender negative trends. It is the duty of all musicians and culturally creative persons to do everything in their power to optimize the processes that are under way and to render them as beneficial as possible to everyone living on our planet.

Benno Signitzer and Pierre Wallnöfer

Structures of the Phonographic Industry in Austria*

1. Introduction

Phonograms (i.e. records and recorded cassettes[1]), like all other mass media, play an increasingly significant role in the modern industrial states. This statement relates, on the one hand, to the growing importance of leisure time, which constitutes a considerable economic factor, and on the other hand to world-wide trends of social development, which some characterize as a transition from a "production" society to an "information" society[2]. In Austria, we find similar indications with the "classical" mass media: a lot of research-work has been done in this field; as concerns the phonograms, however, only sporadic efforts have been made so far. This may, among others, be due to the fact that so far no science has laid claim to this field, or that access to data is extremely difficult (insufficient statistics; tendency to withhold information on the part of the industry). And this is why great hopes are pinned on the research project "Stock-taking of Music Life in Austria" initiated by

---

* Research for this paper was finished in October 1979.

[1] One remark concerning terminology: generally, the term "phonogram" is used in this paper; in some instances, however, it is replaced by "record" – which should be interpreted in such a way as to include the recorded cassette as well.

[2] A leading representative of this school of thought is Daniel Bell, a Harvard sociologist; Cf.: Bell, Daniel, The Coming of Post-Industrial Society, London, Heinemann 1974; Cf. also: Porat, Marc Uri, The Information Economy: Definition and Measurement, U.S. Department of Commerce, Office of Telecommunications, May 1977. For an analysis of the Austrian situation see: Schmoranz, Ingo, "Makroökonomische Analyse des Informationssektors", second interim report; Vienna, Institut für höhere Studien, November 1978. Schmoranz has found that in 1976 32.2% of all Austrian employees worked in the field of information.

Professor Blaukopf, Mediacult Vienna; this project constitutes the first ambitious attempt at an interdisciplinary approach to this field[3].

The subsequent paper aims at describing, with the aid of the data collected so far, some characteristics of the Austrian phonograph market. Production, distribution, consumption, and some aspects of a conceivable cultural policy will be dealt with.

2. Production

Austria's phonographic industry is dominated by nine firms which are all owned by foreign companies[4]. In 1960 they were formed into a cartel, whose market share is currently estimated at 75%.

Shares of the Cartel Firms in the 1978 Cartel Turnover

Firm/owner/country of origin	Turnover share in %
1. Polydor/Philips, Siemens/Netherlands, Federal Republic of Germany	27.8
2. Ariola/Bertelsman AG./Federal Republic of Germany	17.1
3. Phonogram/Philips, Siemens/Netherlands, Federal Republic of Germany	13.4
4. EMI-Columbia, Great Britain	12.1
5. Musica/Decca, Telefunken/Great Britain, Federal Republic of Germany	9.5
6. CBS/Columbia Broadcasting System/U.S.A.	8.1
7. Amadeo/Philips, Siemens/Netherlands, Federal Republic of Germany	7.3
8. Bellaphon/Bellaphon Records GmbH/Federal Republic of Germany	3.9
9. WEA/WEA International/U.S.A.	3.4

Source: Rosenberger, Werner, Marktanteile 1978. Musik in Prozenten. In: Elektro, Radio, Handel No. 5/1979, p. 40.

---

[3] Cf.: Blaukopf, Kurt, Musikland Österreich. Zum Projekt einer Bestandsaufnahme des gegenwärtigen Umgangs mit Musik. In: Mitteilungen des Instituts für Wissenschaft und Kunst, 33rd volume, No. 3/1978; Blaukopf, Kurt, Massenmedium Schallplatte. Die Stellung des Tonträgers in der Kultursoziologie und Kulturstatistik, Wiesbaden 1977.

[4] The structure of the present report is based mainly on the chapter "Schallplatte und MusiCassette" from the book "Massenmedien in Österreich" published in 1977 by the "Salzburger Institut für Publizistik und Kommunikationswissenschaft". This so-called "Media report 1976" contains a number of data to and including the year 1975. Beyond this year, all data were newly collected. Cf.: Signitzer, Benno, et al., Massenmedien in Österreich, Vienna: Internationale Publikationen 1977, pp. 137 – 143.

For over twenty years now the record cartel has played a leading role in the phonogram market; in the past years, however, there have been clear tendencies towards a disintegration of this cartel. The "Marktregelungs-vertrag der österreichischen Schallplattenerzeuger" (market regulation agreement of the Austrian record producers) of 1977 guaranteed a temporary prolongation; but now (October 1979) all signs clearly indicate that the cartel will cease to exist by the end of the year.

Werner Rosenberger, insider and journalist in this field, takes the following view: (... With the termination of the cartel) "the times of prices that are not binding, of fixed rebates, and of common premiums could come to a formal end..." The general disillusionment with the cartel is caused by the present market situation: two years ago, it was feared that the new price system could bring about not only price reductions but a total disintegration of the price structure – not it is realized that not even the cartel could prevent this trend. It was especially parallel imports, foreign goods that were sold cheaply on the market, that gradually permeated the price structure of phonographs, thus encroaching upon the predominance of our domestic industry. Ever since then, the price recommendations have become a farce and had to give way to individual, market-orientated calculations[5].

Phonogram Turnover of the Cartel Firms in Million Austrian Schillings (1972, 1975, 1978)

Phonogram		1972	1975	1978
Single	absolute	60.836	47.925	79.042
	in %	22.8	11.1	11.8
LP	absolute	164.643	253.783	371.753
	in %	61.7	59.0	55.51
MC	absolute	41.327	128.493	218.819
	in %	15.5	29.9	32.67
Total		266.807	430.201	669.614

Source: Signitzer, Benno, et al., Massenmedien in Österreich, ibid. p. 138 and Elektro, Radio, Handel, No. 4/1979, p. 34.

The above table shows that the phonographic industry had a period of expansion in the 1970's: total sales (singles, LP's, and MC's) almost tripled between 1972 and 1978, with the biggest growth rates in the first

---

[5] Rosenberger, Werner, Tonträgermarkt. Kartell kaputt? In: Elektro, Radio, Handel No. 9/1979, p. 74.

half of that period. The latest data, however, whose importance and significance have yet to be corroborated, point to a certain stagnation that has recently come up (1979). A further characteristic of sales developments in the seventies is the dramatic expansion of the cassette as a serious rival to the LP: in the period mentioned, the MC's share in the turnover was more than doubled. As to sales of singles, the situation seems to have stabilized now after a marked downward trend at the beginning of this decade. It should be mentioned, however, that the overall development in the phonogram sector is no doubt determined by the LP and the MC.

2. Firms Not Belonging to the Cartel

In addition to the nine firms forming the Austrian record cartel and representing a market share of about 75%, there exist 30-odd smaller, mainly Austrian firms (e.g. Preiser, Music 2000, Wien-Melodie, Tyrolis), offering mainly Austrian folk music; their market share is estimated at $5-10\%$ (these figures on relative market shares are just rough estimates because of insufficient statistical material). The lion's share of non-cartel sales goes, however, to the so-called TV merchandisers. The two leaders are K-Tel (USA) and Arcade (UK), with a joint market share of about 15%. This constitutes an extraordinary growth rate when compared with a mere 2% in 1976. This new form of distribution, characterized (1) by a clever mix of already successful material, and (2) by exclusive concentration on aggressive radio and TV advertising, has had a strong impact on the Austrian phonogram market, with the result that also cartel firms have started to use this new marketing strategy. This opens up new and interesting perspectives for media impact research, especially with a view to the interaction of several media (media mix; inter-media relations). Taking K-Tel as an example, several characteristics of "merchandising" can be illustrated. K-Tel operates, e.g. with reduced margins for the trade (23% instead of the usual 40%), large circulations (break-even-point at $30-35.000$ pieces), cheap, "recycled" material, and unconventional sales outlets (e.g. filling stations and food shops).

When making a rough breakdown of the Austrian phonogram market according to contents, the following picture evolves: 55% of the turnover is made with "international pop", 30% with "national pop" (presumably mainly folk-music), and 15% with "classical music" (a rather high percentage when compared with the international situation — in the USA the percentage is $5-8$)[6]. Unfortunately no further detailed breakdown as to contents can be made since the statistical material available is rather

---

[6] Figures from the year 1977; classification from: Deutschlands rundy. Musik und Mediennachrichten Vol. 4, January 22, 1978, p. 2.

poor. The data provided by individual cartel firms lead to the following conclusions: Musica, for instance, have a very high percentage (40%) of classical music; CBS and WEA, on the other hand, put great emphasis on international pop (about 70%); Bellaphon stress jazz, which amounts to 25% of their sales. It goes without saying that these figures are by no means complete; an exact contents analysis of the Austrian phonogram market is yet to be made.

Finally, it should be mentioned that the problem of pirated editions and counterfeits, which has existed on international markets for years, has also left its imprints on Austria. Those concerned talk about an annual loss of about 2.5 million Austrian Schillings in copyrights and about 5 million in licenses for interpreters and producers[7].

3. Distribution

Records and cassettes are distributed mainly through retailers and specialized dealers. About 73% of all sales were made through these channels in 1977; this means that figures have dropped when compared with previous years (79.1% in 1975). The wholesalers' share, on the other hand, has increased from a mere 6% in 1975 to 12.5% in 1977. The four largest wholesalers are: "Sonotrade", "Discotrade", "Burkl", and "Music 2000". Their total turnover amounted to approximately 200 million Austrian Schillings in 1978, which corresponds to a unit sale of about 2.2 million. The remaining sales outlets are book-clubs (7.5%, with a slight upward trend), rack-jobbing (1.2%, with a definite downward trend), and the TV merchandisers (17 − 20%)[8].

The process of change that companies and production have undergone over the past years is also noticeable in the field of distribution, but it is much less pronounced. The retailers and specialized dealers can still hold their own as the main channels of distribution; there are, however, other methods that have been successfully established on the market: direct imports, which were made by as many as 15 firms in 1977, have definitely gained in importance[9]. Book clubs, too, have become active in this field; their attraction has increased recently, probably because they can now include hits in their repertory within a very reasonable period of time.

---

[7] Unger, H. C.: Illegale Plattenbrüder. In: Wochenpresse Vol. 34, No. 34, 1979, p. 20.

[8] Baumann, Gunther: Schallplattenumsätze 1977. Fachhandelsanteil sinkt. In: Elektro, Radio, Handel No. 4/1978, pp. 30 − 31. The merchandisers' share of 17 − 20% and the mentioned share of 15% are both estimates used by the trade press.

[9] Baumann, Gunther: Direktimporteure (I): Marktmacht mangelt noch. In: Elektro, Radio, Handel No. 8/1977, p. 24.

Moreover, book clubs cater to new customers especially in fields with a poorly developed retail infrastructure.

Rack-jobbing on the other hand, which has become so successful in other countries (the USA, for instance), could not make any decisive inroads into the established structures despite a promising start.

4. Consumption

The importance of the record as a mass medium, which was stressed at the beginning of this paper, is clearly shown by the position it takes as regards consumption and leisure time. According to the 1976 media analysis, 37.5% of all Austrians between 14 and 70 years of age mentioned listening to records and cassettes when asked about their hobbies. With the 20 − 29 year-olds, this percentage rises to 50. 750 million Austrian Schillings were spent on phonograms in 1975[10].

A study made by the Fessel Institute in 1976 underlines the unchallenged position that listening to music (including the radio) holds among the leisure-time activities pursued at home:

Listening to Music as the Most Frequent Leisure-Time Activity Pursued at Home Was Mentioned by:

Pupils	67.6%
Apprentices	72.9%
Technical college students	85.4%
Grammar school students	67.3%
Students	69.9%
Salaried employees	71.0%
Skilled workers	66.0%
Other workers	68.0%
Young people in the country	66.0%
Young people in the cities	78.0%

Source: Mörth, I., Problembereich und Zielgruppe der Jugendarbeit. Freizeit, Familie und Arbeitsbereich als Spannungsfelder von Jugend und Gesellschaft in Österreich. In: Report Forschung, Information, published by the "Österreichisches Institut für Jugendkunde" No. 12/1977, pp. 32 − 36.

5. Summary and Prospects for the Future

The data on the structure of the Austrian phonographic industry presented here in a nutshell indicate a general increase in production over the past decade, but they also show strong trends toward concentration and a surprisingly great dependency on foreign markets. The three firms

---

[10] Österreichische Autorenzeitung No. 2/1976, p. 9.

forming the "Polygram-Gruppe" — owned by Philips (Netherlands) and Siemens (Federal Republic of Germany) — share about half the sales of the Austrian cartel phonograms.

The nine big companies making up the so-called record cartel all have their parent firms abroad. Their market share lies around 75%. A further characteristic of the Austrian phonogram situation is the far-reaching structural change in the industry that has taken place over the past years, and it is quite impossible at present to predict its exact impact on future developments. The record cartel that has dominated the development of the Austrian phonographic industry for the past 21 years is on the verge of dissolution; and for quite some years now — long before its predicted termination on Dec. 31, 1979 — there has been a steady decline in market shares. This structural change did, however, not strengthen the domestic Austrian production. This is clearly shown by the fact that the decline of the cartel runs parallel to the dramatic upsurge of direct imports and of foreign TV merchandisers (K-Tel, Arcade).

In the course of the past decade, media and communication policy has become increasingly important in the field of political activity — especially as regards the social aspects of the so-called "classical" media, namely radio and press (as examples may serve: press- and magazine subsidies and promotion; the media law; re-organization of Austrian radio and TV). With phonograms, there have been no such tendencies so far. This may be due to the fact that, as initially mentioned, this topic has seen only sporadic scientific initiatives in Austria so far — let it be by journalism, publishing or other disciplines.

So far, the phonogram has not been included in the media-political programmes of the political parties, pressure groups, and the churches[11]. And yet such programmes (on governmental as well as non-governmental levels) seem to be legitimate and desirable when considering the social significance of records and cassettes (as an economic factor, and in fields such as leisure time, education, etc.). It is said that systematic political

---

[11] There is, for example, no mention of phonograms in the media-political concept of the SPÖ (Austrian Socialist Party) published in 1974 ("Medien, Presse, Film, Hörfunk und Fernsehen, neue elektronische Medien, Agenturen, Verlagswesen, Buch. Bericht der Medienkommission an den Bundestag der SPÖ", February 1974). The media concept presented by the Austrian People's Party [ÖVP] in 1979 ("Neue Wege für Österreich. Liberale Medienpolitik", Vienna: ÖVP 1979) does contain a chapter on "Buch, Schallplatte, Kassette und Verlage" (pp. 19 – 22), phonograms are, however, given only superficial treatment. Moreover, the authors of this paper do not know of any media-political statements on this topic by the ÖGB (Austrian Trade Union Congress), the Bundeswirtschaftskammer (Federal Chamber of Commerce), the Church or any other social pressure group.

action is often brought about by dramatic changes or by a crisis – should this really be true then the dramatic change that is about to occur in the phonographic industry at the end of the seventies might become extremely significant. The economic development of the phonogram is, just like that of all other media, closely interrelated with the development of new technologies (digital phonograms, video discs, etc.).

What now are the topics that the new media and cultural policy for phonograms would have to deal with? Three aspects should serve as an illustration: First, there is the problem of strong dependency on foreign companies – a problem that holds true for many Austrian media. If we consider the record not as an exclusively commercial product but rather as a means to convey cultural assets and to unite nations, the promotion of a genuine Austrian production and of a rather free and mutual international exchange does gain in importance. One could envisage such promotional efforts as have been made so far for magazines and for scientific and literary publications. That way, the great disadvantage of a rather small Austrian market could – at least partly – be balanced off. The aim of such policy would therefore not be chauvinist isolation but rather a qualitative improvement of international relations and exchange, with special emphasis on a genuine plurality of all countries concerned.

A further goal of such a "phonogram policy" could consist in decentralizing existing structures. Regional, sub-regional, and local programmes that are directed intentionally at only a limited audience should be promoted. The many small Austrian firms not belonging to the cartel (see item 2) could no doubt form the basis of decentralized production. This aspect, too, coincides with the efforts by radio, TV, and press aiming at efficient decentralization.

A third field of activity could try to adapt the principle of "participatory communication" to the phonogram, especially the cassette. In addition to the passive consumption of recorded cassettes, this medium could also comprise active productions by the audience. For many years now film and photo cameras have become media of active personal expression for the broad public – could blank cassettes and tapes not also be used for individual and group communication? This would open up a new field for youth and adult education, emphasizing the creative use of one's leisure time.

And finally it must be stated that neither a structural analysis of the Austrian phonographic industry nor the formulation and implementation of successful social policies are feasible without more pronounced emphasis on scientific findings and research methods. But – and here we come back to where we started from – only sporadic efforts have been made so far in this field.

Helmut Steinmetz

Copyright, Neighbouring Rights, and Piracy in Austria

1. General Remarks

Considering the variety of angles from which the subject of phonograms and cultural communication is being treated within the framework of this Seminar, it would also seem interesting to examine the position of the modern constitutional state with respect to cultural and in particular musical creation and interpretation as well as to the phonogram as one of its major media of communication.

Since all modern industrialized countries in East and West protect intellectual creations in the fields of music, literature, the plastic arts and cinematography — admittedly to varying degrees — but in principle without exception, it seems justified to conclude that this legal protection is generally regarded as the condition and the means of preserving and developing the creative potential of mankind. Thus, the initial question, whether artistic creation stands at all in need of being protected by the state legal systems can be clearly answered in the affirmative and we may turn to a more detailed discussion of the forms and the efficacy of protection. With certain modifications, Austria may be taken as an example of the situation in the other West European countries.

In Austria, state protection of cultural achievements has been embodied in the Copyright Act [Urheberrechtsgesetz], whose essential provisions date back to 1936. In retrospect and measured by the standards of the time this act may be regarded as very progressive, already combining the protection of cultural creations, that is to say "copyright" in the narrow sense, with the protection of neighbouring rights, in particular the rights of performing artists and phonogram producers, to mention only the most important fields touching upon our subject. This act was supplemented by the act on copyright administration societies, also from the year 1936, which contains regulations concerning the then most topical form of mass communication of cultural works, namely the broadcasting and performing rights subsisting in the so-called small musical works.

2. Protection of the Work

For the protection of his intellectual and material interests the legal system grants to the author the general right to prohibit any kind of unauthorized use. Anybody wishing to make use of the work must, therefore, ask the author's permission, which enables the latter to make his assent dependent on certain conditions, to limit the permission as to content, time or territory and, not last, to demand royalties. The author's rights are further safeguarded by being in principle non-transferable, except by interstate succession; granted can only be exploitation rights which are called "Werknutzungsrechte" (rights to exploit a work), if they are exclusive, and "Werknutzungsbewilligungen" (permissions to exploit a work), if they are not exclusive. In addition these rights are construed as so-called absolute rights, i.e. as rights that are effective with respect to third parties at any time and place. A bona fide acquisition of such rights is impossible.

2.1 Economic Rights

The protection of the author's material interests is guaranteed by the so-called exploitation rights that are all based on the principle of giving the author an equitable share in the returns from his work. In practice, the author's material claim will, as a rule, not become effective at the level of direct use of a work but at the level of communication. It is, for instance, not the purchaser of the phonogram who pays the author's royalties but the phonogram manufacturer.

The economic protection rights comprise:

> the reproduction right
> the distribution right
> the broadcasting right
> the right of public performance and communication.

By reserving these rights to the author, he can also decide whether his work shall be made accessible to the public or not.

2.2 Protection of Moral Rights ("Droit Moral")

As only "personal intellectual creations" are copyrightable (§1, Copyright Act) or, in other words, achievements that bear the imprint of the creator's personality and individuality, the legal system has also to protect the author's moral rights.

This is provided for by:

> the right of authorship (unrenounceable right)
> right to be named
> protection against cuts, additions, modifications,
> and distortion of the work or the title.

2.3 Limitations of Copyright

The comment on the Austrian copyright act from 1936 states: "Public interest in cultural development obviously calls for effective protection of the author, while at the same time requiring measures preventing copyright from becoming a hindrance to this development." This conflict of interests is resolved in all effective copyright acts by provisions about the so-called "fair uses", such as duplication for personal use, free use of quotations, the liberty of creating musical settings, free current-affairs reporting, free use for school song books, etc. In addition, the absolute right to prohibit the reproduction and dissemination of musical works on phonograms is subject to compulsory licences to anybody interested, once a licence to record has been granted by the person entitled. Thus, in the phonogram sector, there exist no exclusive exploitation rights in musical works.

As far as free duplication for personal use goes, one has to add that the act of the year 1936 naturally could not foresee that in the 60s and 70s of our century technology would enable any private person, by simply pressing a button, to produce a recording of a musical work on a sound carrier, whose quality is essentially equal to that of the industrial product. Modern technical equipment, like the cassette recorder and now also the video recorder, has opened up a vast field for private recording and re-recording, which according to current regulations is largely permissible without the author's licence. In our economic reality this means an acute threat to the production and distribution of industrial phonograms, which is most clearly evidenced by the fact that in Austria, just as in the other industrial countries of the Western world, annual sales of blank cassettes are three times those of recorded musicassettes. Internationally speaking, the only approach to a solution was made in the Federal Republic of Germany in 1966, in the form of a levy, currently amounting to about 4%, on the manufacturer's or importer's returns from recording equipment. In the Federal Republic this solution has meanwhile come to be regarded as unsatisfactory and one is now demanding a surcharge on blank tapes. No such regulations are in force in any of the other countries. In Austria, for instance, one has tried for more than 10 years to get a regulation similar to that in the Federal Republic, but so far a relevant amendment to the copyright act has been prevented by the industry.

3. Protection of Neighbouring Rights

3.1 Protection of Performing Artists

When a performer presents a literary or musical work, this performance may only be recorded, duplicated and disseminated on a sound carrier, transmitted on radio or communicated to the public, with his permission. As in the case of copyright, this right of prohibition is restricted by fair use in the public interest (cf. Pt. 2.3). In the case of broadcasts and communication to the public of a performance already recorded on a phonogram, the right of prohibition is moreover mitigated to a mere claim to remuneration, which in the case of a broadcast can only be enforced via the manufacturer of the phonogram and in the case of communication to the public via the organizer. On the other hand, the provision for compulsory licence does not apply to the performing artist in the case of phonogram productions, so that he may, and frequently does grant exclusive rights of exploitation.

To protect his intellectual interests, the performing artist has the right to decide whether and in what form he is to be named on the phonogram.

3.2 Protection of the Producer of Phonograms

Whoever records acoustic events on a sound carrier ("producer") is protected by law against unauthorized duplication of this sound carrier. In the case of commercially produced phonograms the owner of the enterprise is considered the producer. In contrast to the rights of performing artists, the acoustic event need not be related to a copyrightable literary or musical work, but may also concern a non-copyrightable event. If a phonogram produced for commercial purposes is broadcast or communicated to the public, the law does not provide for a prohibition right, but merely for a claim to remuneration, which, in the absence of any other agreement, the phonogram producer shares on a fifty-fifty basis with the performing artist.

The rights of phonogram producers are again restricted by provisions safeguarding the public interest, in particular by the right of duplication for personal use.

4. Copyright Terms

In order to resolve the conflict of interests between the claim of the creative or re-creative person to the protection of his achievement and the public interest in free access to cultural creations, the mentioned copyrights and neighbouring rights are of limited duration, in Austria as well as in all the other countries.

The Austrian copyright act provides for the following copyright terms:

4.1 The copyright in literary and musical works expires 70 years after the author's death.

4.2 Exploitation rights of performing artists expire 50 years after the end of the year in which the performance was given.

4.3 The protection of phonograms expires 50 years after the date of recording or publication.

5. Sanctions

Of the civil-law sanctions against infringements of the above outlined rights we should mention the claim to injunctive relief, to elimination of the unlawful situation and destruction of the illegally produced copy, the claim to publication of court decisions, to equitable compensation as well as to damages and recovery of the profit in case of culpable damage. Penal-law sanctions presuppose intentional infringement and provide for fines up to 360 "daily rates"[1] or up to 6 months' imprisonment. In addition there is the possibility of confiscation and again the claim to have the products and means of infringement destroyed or rendered unfit for use. Under the terms of the Austrian law, copyright infringements are treated as petty offences, which means that the injured party has to bring action for criminal prosecution within 6 weeks of getting knowledge of the infringement, being fully liable for costs in case of acquittal. It further means that the state considers the unlawfulness of record piracy to be equal to that of an insult to someone's honour. I am sure that no further comment is called for.

6. International Perspective

Copyright and neighbouring rights are subject to the so-called principle of territoriality, i.e. the conditions for the protection of a work or an achievement are determined by and limited to the jurisdiction of the respective national legal system, which also defines to what extent and on what conditions works and achievements of foreign citizens shall enjoy this protection. The protection of foreigners may either be effected through bilateral state treaties, which nowadays are of subordinate importance, or through multilateral conventions.

6.1 The two most important international copyright treaties are:

---

[1] A fine under Austrian law, computed on the basis of the offender's income.

6.1.1 *The Bern Convention* of 1886, with the revisions of Paris 1896, Berlin 1908, Bern 1914, Rome 1928, Brussels 1948 (the version valid in Austria), Stockholm 1967, and Paris 1971. This international convention, which is characterized by providing a high degree of protection and which rejects any formal filing requirements as a prerequisite to protection, currently comprises 71 countries, including practically all modern industrial states, with the exception of the USA and the Soviet Union.

6.1.2 The Universal Copyright Convention adopted in Geneva in 1952 and revised in Paris in 1971. The version valid in Austria, is that of 1952. This convention provides a much lower level of protection. Any formal filing requirements of national legal systems are deemed fulfilled, if the works of foreign nationals bear the symbol © accompanied by the name of the copyright owner and the year of first publication. This convention is currently adhered to by 72 countries as well as the United States and the Soviet Union (since May 27, 1973).

6.2 In the field of neighbouring rights a much lower degree of international standardization of national legal systems has been achieved. The basis was to be provided by the Rome agreement of 1961, which relates to the protection of performers, producers of phonograms and of broadcasting organizations. So far, only 21 countries, including Austria (since 1973) adhere to this agreement.

In consequence, the International Convention for the protection of producers of phonograms against unauthorized duplication of their phonograms (the so-called Geneva Piracy Convention) was adopted in 1971, which is now adhered to by 32 countries, but not by Austria. Another special agreement to be mentioned is the Brussels Satellite Convention of 1974 as well as diverse Council-of-Europe agreements, mostly concerned with the rights of broadcasting organizations.

7. Copyright Administration Societies

It was mentioned earlier that the Austrian legislators passed an act providing for so-called copyright administration societies, as early as in 1936. In doing so they were guided by the realization, currently gaining ground, that copyright and neighbouring rights will largely remain a nudum jus, if no supporting measures are taken that regulate the practical exercise of those rights in the interest of both the author and the user. Already in 1936, the Austrian law provided for a state-controlled copyright administration society concerned with the exercise of the rights of public performance and broadcasts subsisting in musical works [AKM, Staatlich genehmigte Gesellschaft der Autoren, Komponisten und Musikverleger] and a society concerned with the same rights in the literary sector [LVG, Staatlich genehmigte literarische Verwertungsgesellschaft], which has, however, failed to gain any practical importance with respect to broadcasting rights. New technical developments led to the formation of further organizations, namely of AUSTRO-MECHANA for mechanical reproduction rights in musical works, the LITERAR-MECHANA for mechanical reproduction rights in literary works and the society for the protection of neighbouring rights [LSG, Wahrnehmung von Leistungs-schutzrechten Ges.m.b.H.], concerned with the rights and claims to remuneration of performing artists and phonogram producers. Endeavours are currently being made to put the last named societies and the already existing society for the rights of visual artists [VBK, Verwertungs-gesellschaft bildender Künstler] as well as the society for cinematographic rights, which is just being formed, under state control and to stipulate the obligation to contract and protection of the monopolistic position.

8. Piracy

"Laws are made to be broken", seems to be the motto of phonogram piracy, which has one common denominator to all its different forms, namely the fact that phonograms are illegally produced and distributed.

8.1 Bootlegs

The term bootlegs or underground records refers to unauthorized recordings made of concert and opera performances as well as of radio or even TV-transmissions or to the unauthorized exploitation of studio tapes. The term goes back to the Prohibition in the United States, when moonshined whisky had to be smuggled in bootlegs. Bootleg records can usually be recognized by their outer appearance, being sold in simple white sleeves with a mimeographed sheet informing about contents inserted between sleeve and cellophane cover. The labels are black or white, bearing either the indications "Side One" and "Side Two" or typical phantasy names, like Dragonfly Records, Idle Mind Productions, Pig's Eye, The Amazing Kornyphon Records, etc., which are well-known to the insider. In the pop-music sector a special catalogue, called Hot Wacks, is circulating, which has gone through 7 editions and lists more than 1000 different bootlegs, with average sales of at least 2000.

Some of them, such as Bob Dylan's "Great White Wonder" would long have been gilded on the legal market.

For the so-called "serious music" sector there exist specialized mail-order firms, like "Mr. Tape" in New York, that transact business only via constantly changing post boxes. They offer illegal, direct recordings of almost all interesting opera performances given in Europe and America over the past 20 years, either made directly at the opera houses or from broadcasts. The manufacturers of bootlegs acquire no rights in the composition, no rights in the texts and pay no licence fees to the performer or, when utilizing existing tapes, to the producer of these tapes, or to the broadcasting organization, when utilizing a broadcast. The share of bootlegs in total piracy sales is probably below 10%.

8.2 Counterfeits

A form of piracy that in some countries has assumed alarming proportions is the slavish imitation of an industrial phonogram, which means that a phonogram is re-recorded and the lable as well as the cover or the inlay card is photographically imitated, which makes it particularly difficult to trace and discover these products. Besides infringing the rights of composers, text writers, phonogram manufacturers, and performing artists, they often violate the unfair trade law, the law of trademarks, the law protecting patterns and designs and in addition constitute criminal offences such as fraud and receiving of stolen goods.

8.3 Special Forms

Cases of piracy, in which a combination of hits is offered on MC, which legally is not available on one single phonogram could be called "unauthentic counterfeits".

A particularly subtle form of piracy is "overproduction". The manufacturer simply produces from the masters more units than ordered. The overproduction is sold illegally. Mention ought finally to be made of cassettes recorded by private persons and sold to friends or through newspaper ads, to increase their tax-free incomes.

8.4 Total Volume

The attached list, which represents the world-wide volume of phonogram piracy on the basis of 1977, and was drawn up by the International Federation of Producers of Phonograms and Videograms (IFPI/London), goes to show that piracy sales are already hitting the life nerve of the phonographic industry. For the current year, total world-wide sales of pirated phonograms, based on the end consumer price, are estimated to reach 1,000 million dollars.

8.5 Austria

In Austria, pirated phonograms are assumed to hold a market share of 2 to 3%, but even this fortunately modest degree of piracy reaches the tune of 30 to 40 million AS, measured by a total market volume, based on the end consumer price, of currently about 1,400 million AS. The loss in royalties resulting from these sales must be estimated at a minimum of 2 to 2 1/2 million AS, the losses incurred by performers and phonogram producers at more than double that amount.

Although, as mentioned above, the Austrian copyright act provides for both civil-law and penal-law sanctions against the infringement of copyrights and neighbouring rights, enormous amounts of money, time and energy have to be invested in the fight against piracy. Austria, as a country with a relatively small domestic production and high imports, is a typical import country also in the piracy sector. Therefore, the tracing and discovery of pirated material depends largely on a fast and well-organized exchange of information and on detailed knowledge of delivery channels. Since pirated products are often mixed with original ones it is very rarely possible to prove any intentional offence on the part of the importer or dealer. Our requests to have the Copyright Act amended to the effect that also gross negligence will be subject to legal sanctions, have thus far not been met by the state authorities.

So we must hope against hope that gradually the general public will come to understand that the theft of the creative achievements of others is no mere peccadillo, but will in the long run deal a deathblow to cultural creation.

It is for us to join forces in fighting this threat.

Volume of Piracy 1977

Unauthorized Duplication of Records and Tapes

Area	Units (in millions)	Value (million US $)
North America	70.0	335.0
South America	12.5	25.0
Europe	38.0	100.0
Middle East and Africa	40.0	100.0
South East Asia and Australasia	250.0	220.0
Estimated value worldwide		780.0

Country	Units (in millions)	Value (million US $)	% of market (tape market)	
Australia	1.0	3.3		(3%)
Belgium	1.25	3.5		(10%)
Brasil	2.5	10.0		(35%)
Canada	4.3	8.0	5%	
France	2.5	7.5	5%	
Germany	5.0	38.0	5%	(8%)
Great Britain	1.5	3.75		(5%)
Greece	8.0	15.0		(80%)
Hongkong	12.0	10.0		(80%)
Indonesia	120.0	90.0		(99%)
Israel	75.0	150.0		(50%)
Italy	8.0	20.0		(50%)
Malaysia	25.0	26.0	90%	
Mexico	4.2	8.8		(25%)
Netherlands	2.8	8.0	10%	
Nigeria	5.0	10.0		(75%)
Philippines	5.0	10.0	70%	
Portugal	0.5	1.0		(80%)
Singapore	20.0	17.0		(95%)
South Africa	2.75	8.0		(20%)
South Korea	30.0	18.0	80%	(100%)
Spain	0.8	2.0		(10%)
Switzerland	0.6	2.0	5%	
Taiwan	10.0	6.0	90%	
Thailand	20.0	30.0	99%	
Turkey	7.0	16.0		(95%)
U.S.A.	65.0	325.0	10%	(25%)

Wilhelm Schlemm

On the Position of the "Tonmeister" (Sound Recordist) in the Musical Communication Process

Introduction

When discussing the fate of music in the media, one usually departs from a given sound carrier and reflects on the effects on the listener. The genesis of the sound carrier, its problematic position between art and technology, which becomes manifest in the presentation of music by technical means, is as a rule unknown to the outsider. Contrary to a widespread conception, the communication of music through the media is not solely a technical task to be tackled with the help of communication engineering, but implies a number of aesthetic and artistic questions which decisively influence the outcome, i.e. the phonogram that can be reproduced whenever and as often as desired.

There is a growing awareness of the fact that music and technology are not merely an additive combination, with technology acting as vehicle for the musical information, but that the originally passive, subservient role of the medium has been superseded by a functional interpenetration of art and technology. Technology has ceased to be an extrinsic prerequisite of communication and the reproductive qualities of the technical apparatus have become an integral part of the production process. The operation of the technical equipment has become emancipated from a mere service to a joint artistic responsibility and creativity, the medium itself becoming part of the artistic accomplishment. In the following we are going to deal with a) the operational characteristics of the electro-acoustic medium with respect to music, its peculiarities and transformations, and b) a job description of the "Tonmeister" — a new artistic-technical profession evolved from technology — and his role in the musical communication process.

On the Interaction of Music and Technology

The embracement of music by technology has created a new sound reality and has become a matter of course in our musical environment. The experience with electronic music, gathered along with the development of the electro-acoustic medium, the findings of sound analysis made possible by technical devices, as well as the development of electric musical instruments, have left their imprint on both the creation and reproduction of music. They have provided the composer with new sound material and the performing musician with new modes of sound production. With the help of technology pop music has created its own "sound"; though originally bound up with the media, this "sound" has also coined certain forms of live music-making.

The most outstanding technical achievement in this field – the tape recording, reaching its most advanced form in multi-channel techniques – has provided the technical precondition for translating the organization of sound into operations that can only be effected by technical means and which, when compared with conventional music-making and acoustic musical instruments, make the latter appear archaic and primitive.

The much-abused concept of perfection, in itself a technical category, has gained a lasting influence on performing practice, not only in the specific media context but beyond that on music-making in general. Apart from the often deplored surfeit of music programmes offered by the media, one can also observe a heightened perception of musical nuances, which is certainly also due to the media.

The Operational Characteristics of the Medium

Unlike photographs taken of paintings or sculptures, which are called reproductions, the electro-acoustic communication of music reproduces only the rendering or the procedure of performing a work, but not the work itself. In contrasting the term "original" and the term "tinned", linguistic usage neglects the fact that in the case of musical communication there is no original comparable to the original of a painting. The true, though acceptedly ephemeral existence of music starts with its translation into sound. This original state, which is experienced through its development in time, can be produced by both a live and a media representation.

There are three ways in which the medium of electro-acoustic transmission can link a source (e.g. an orchestra) with a receiver (listener); they have developed successively with the progress of technology, but they also exist side by side without any clearcut lines of demarcation. The simplest way is that of *passive transmission*, which occurs when whatever is fed to the medium can be retrieved at the receiving end. A case of passive transmission would be a news broadcast, if one regards nothing but the content of the news, whose meaning remains unchanged by its passage through the transmission chain. When the object of transmission is music, the medium assumes a different function. In the case of music it is also a question of how something is transmitted, i.e. which are the essential sound qualities communicated, and how it is to be listened to.

The result of a transmission depends on the relation that is established between the transmission apparatus and the object of transmission. In this type of *evaluating transmission* the medium can be manipulated both in favour of the source and with a view to listeners' expectations. The manipulation is a subjective act of the person handling the medium.

An advanced form is that of *active transmission*, with the apparatus analytically penetrating the sound event, extracting differently rated partial aspects from the sonic totality and transforming them by way of the medium into a sound synthesis with new qualities. The resulting loudspeaker output still resembles the original situation but is no longer identical with it. The medium communicates the idea of a wôrk, but transforms its sonic shape.

The active character of the medium is enhanced by the possibility offered by the equipment of influencing the evolution of sound with respect to time (recording and subsequent editing/synchronization), tone quality (balance, filtering, reverberation) and spatial parameters (panorama, presence, gradation from front to back).

Today's pop music (which is meant to include whatever is not counted as so-called serious music) knows a great number of specific sound effects, triggered either by the player (e.g. Wah-wah, Fuzz, Leslie, etc.) or inserted during the mixing process, when the sound pattern receives its final shape (e.g. Shatter, Phasing, Harmonizer, Vocoder, a.o.), for which the performers with their conventional instrumental or vocal means have, as it were, merely supplied the sonic raw material. The previously clear-cut separation between source and medium, that is between the sound-generating instrument and the pick-up apparatus, becomes increasingly blurred and is totally obliterated by electronic musical instruments such as the synthesizer.

The current multi-track technique permits not only freedom in the production process (synchronization), taking account of certain commercial coercions, but also creates the conditions for a sound separation, which makes for the characteristic "sound" of this type of music, by facilitating the above mentioned analytical penetration. In this way instruments and parts with the most diverse sound volumes can be "processed" together to create an artificial tonality that is impossible to accomplish by conventional "natural" means.

As a peculiarity of media sound we note the tendency of rock music to cultivate, as it were, the faults of the technical equipment, rejecting the perfectionism of high-fidelity workshop. The distortion resulting from the overmodulation of individual components of a transmission is considered a constituent feature of the rock sound. This, if no other phenomenon, invalidates the time-honoured conception of a neutral communication, i.e. reproduction, of music through the medium.

Job Description of the "Tonmeister"

Sound control, as it has evolved from the available equipment, is personified by the "Tonmeister". It is a relatively young profession, which in Germany appeared with the sound film and with broadcasting in the 20s. Already in those early days, training courses were held which concentrated on the latest findings of acoustics. In a report from 1935 it says that the "Tonmeister" should not be an engineer with some musical knowledge, but a musician who has learned to play the technical equipment like an instrument. It was only in 1947 that a systematic course of studies was introduced by Erich Thienhaus at the Acoustics Institute of the Nordwestdeutsche Musikakademie in Detmold. His basic concept was to train "Tonmeister" who would be capable of harmonizing technical and musical aspects in the recording of music.

But the "Tonmeister's" scope of activities is not restricted to music productions; it embraces all art forms that are totally or partly presented by acoustic means (radio play, feature, film, television, theatre). In the present paper, however, priority is given to the music production.

Within the field of sound recording, processing and transmission we currently come up against a confusing variety of names and titles, a fact which is referable to the separate development of and diverse tasks to be fulfilled in the individual media. Attempts are made to subsume the professions of Aufnahmeleiter, Produktionsleiter, Programmingenieur, Toningenieur, Synchrontonmeister, Misch-Tonmeister, Tonregisseur, Musikregisseur, etc. under the term "Tonmeister", on the condition that the mentioned titles refer to activities identified in the job description of the "Tonmeister", issued by the Bundesanstalt für Arbeit (Federal Labour Institute) in Nuremberg in agreement with the Verband Deutscher Tonmeister (Association of German Sound Recordists).

The main point of this job description is to outline the "Tonmeister's" complex scope of activities and to spot the features that are common to the different professional branches, in order to promote an understanding of the problems peculiar to the profession (including the question of recruitment) among outsiders and to facilitate an evaluation.

To understand the problems one has first of all to acknowledge the profession's novel constellation between art and technology, the line of demarcation being drawn between technical service and artistic representation with the help of technical means. The term "Tonmeister" is intended to signal the creative, artistic component of this profession.

Used in this sense, the term "Tonmeister" has even been adopted outside the German-speaking area. The University of Surrey/England, for instance, runs a "Tonmeister degree course".

The theoretical job description, however, is confronted with the current job practice. So far, one has neither succeeded in making the scope of activities of the "Tonmeister" sufficiently transparent to the public (which includes staff managers of companies and institutions, department heads, employer organizations and trade unions), nor has it been possible to bring the intended standardization of the title of "Tonmeister" in harmony with the conditions developed in the course of time and now prevailing among the various professional groups and with the different organizational patterns. The Bayerischer Rundfunk has been the first and so far the only broadcasting organization in Germany to introduce the title "Tonmeister" and to abolish previously used synonyms.

Things are rendered even more difficult by the double meaning of some of the titles currently in use. In the phonographic industry a "Tonmeister" is the same as a "Toningenieur" in radio. The "Toningenieur" in radio (whose opposite number in television is called "Bildingenieur") is in charge of all kinds of sound engineering tasks from broadcasting operations to maintenance service. Given the required training or acquired skill, the title of "Toningenieur" is further up in the hierarchy than that of "Tontechniker". Besides, specially qualified "Toningenieure" (the qualification derives from their practical work) are employed in the special sound engineering sectors of music, radio play and feature production. These are considered to be the most demanding tasks. Due to the artistic component of the production tasks, the work of the radio "Toningenieur" belongs to the scope of activities of the "Tonmeister", as outlined in the job description. A "Toningenieur" of this calibre, who, because of his specific tasks is also called "Programmingenieur" or "Produktionsingenieur", belongs normally to the technical department of the radio station and is responsible to the technical directorate.

The majority of those working as "Tonmeister" in radio organizations, whose opposite numbers in the record industry would probably be the "Aufnahmeleiter" or the "Produzent", have passed the courses run in Berlin or Detmold and have undergone systematic musical training. Inside the ARD (Arbeitsgemeinschaft der Rundfunkanstalten Deutschlands) they belong to the music departments and are thus answerable to the programme directorate.

The "Tonmeister" in the production department of an ARD-TV-station also belongs to the administrative scope of the programme directorate, even if his tasks are rather of a technical order, like those of the "Programmingenieur" in radio.

In big record companies and in the radio stations of broadcasting corporations it has proved expedient to have two people in charge in the control room, assisted by auxiliary technical staff ("Tontechniker" etc.). One partner in this team will take care of the more technical tasks, the other of the more artistic ones, but there is no clear division of competence. Together, they accomplish the tasks of sound control. So the difficulty lies not only in understanding the functional interpenetration of art and technology, which according to the above is the essence of sound control, but also in the fact that this is to be jointly accomplished by two persons, whom one would wish to categorize in administrative terms. (The exception is Philips, where the producer is a "one-man team", who in personal union takes care of the mixing console and of the score.) A number of arguments can be put forward in favour of the two-men principle, among others the situation of a live radio broadcast. Still, one cannot rule out the possibility that future production conditions will suggest other staff patterns.

In terms of staff management there remains the discrepancy between the efforts to introduce the common title of "Tonmeister" and the different tasks posed by the job. When discussing pertinent problems, this discrepancy must not be confused with the uniform function of sound control, drawing on both the artistic and technical components: The duality of art and technology, which is reflected in the duality of "Tonmeister" and "Toningenieur" (according to the radio pattern), must be understood as a partnership comparable to the relations between conductor and soloist. This is another case where one can hardly say that the performance of the one is more important than that of the other. In the individual case one will probably be able to claim that the one or the other has taken the lead in this or that situation. But this is a circumstance that is not rooted in the respective function but in the persons forming a team.

In the multitude of smaller (private) studios one will usually find only one person in charge, who according to the job description could very well be counted as "Tonmeister". But if one considers the technical tasks he is burdened with, from equipment maintenance to innovation planning, the "Tonmeister" is in such cases usually more of a "Toningenieur". In a studio that is run as a services enterprise his self-assessment as "Tonmeister", as artistic personality, will be shaken by the conditions prevailing in such undertakings: for a commissioned production the "Tonmeister" is "hired out" to the client just like the studio equipment. The "Tonmeister" is expected to handle the equipment in accordance with the client's every wish and — somehow as an adjunct — to "make" the desired sound. In this he is assisted by the producer or a qualified deputy, often the arranger or bandleader. So, eventually, one has again a team of two.

On the Position of Sound Control and of the "Tonmeister" in the Musical Communication Process

The sophisticated technical equipment and production processes which music and music-making are confronted with in our time, may well be impressing, but they offer no real insight into the process of "mediatization". A minute description of the apparatus will probably show up the possibilites of technical manipulation, but cannot reveal the reasons underlying the aesthetic conception governing its application.

The fascination that may emanate from technical equipment is confronted with the uneasiness of those who are used to think in musical categories. An overestimation of technology, on the one hand, and a resigned lack of understanding, on the other hand, give rise to the entirely wrong notion that everything can be done with a generous helping of technology. The much-used slogan that equipment transmits music better than it can be heard in the concert hall, which is meant to point out the undoubtedly high technical standard of this equipment, should not conceal the essential precondition: the work of the sound control team. The faultless technical functioning of the equipment is a necessary but in itself insufficient precondition of a good transmission. Only when used by a controlling intellect to an artistic end, the equipment becomes meaningful. This applies, even if some technical operations within the entire operational network are mechanized. The use of compressors, for instance, will not solve the difficult problem of dynamics, but will at best help to tackle it more successfully. The current discussion about increased automation of studio operations ought not to be understood in the sense that sound control and thus the work of the "Tonmeister" are dispensable or can be replaced by mechanized equipment. Exactly the opposite is demanded by those practically engaged in the transmission of music, who want increased automation of the routine operations, so as to relieve the "Tonmeister", freeing him for his creative tasks.

The described types of transmission are employed contiguously and are graded according to a given task. In the field of so-called serious music, the use of active transmission attains an interpretative quality which may cover the range between the primary sound production by the musician before the microphone and that which the sound control team believe to be able to derive from the score. This interpretative leeway is related less to the primary musical performance — though in a studio production it may well result from a discussion with the performers – than to the "me-diatized", transformed musical pattern. In the specific situation of an electro-acoustic transmission, which means reduction to the auditive, sound components are accentuated or suppressed to achieve greater distinctness and better reception. By using technical means an aestheti-cally motivated balance is struck between what is primarily, acoustically presented, what is musically intended, what is noticeably indicated as desirable by the score, and what is desirable in terms of reception. This cannot be achieved by "purely" technical handling of the transmission apparatus, nor is the outcome of the transmission the sole achievement of the performers and/or the unadulterated representation of the "primary" interpreter's ideas.

In pop music, which has its very own way of including technical sound effects either before the microphone or by way of the technical com-munication, the function of sound control goes beyond the interpretative, entering the realm of creative organization of sound. This creative function is not limited to the correlation of various sound groups (balance), but also means the introduction of specific sound effects, which are available in almost infinite variety, with unlimited possibilities of variation. Artificial reverberation is certainly still the most remarkable effect; it is either used to correct room acoustics or as a sound ingredient, which makes for density and intensity, but also for volume and freedom of sound.

The function of sound control, as understood from the above, manifests itself only in connection with the artistic performance of others. The performance of the "Tonmeister" is never an isolated end in itself, which makes it difficult to appraise his work. It would certainly be wrong to label it as parasitic – for its seemingly parasitic existence – or, going even further, to define it as cheap technical service. Considering the place value of the phonogram in the musical life of our time, it would certainly be inapposite to regard it as a mere accessory to music-making. One has to realize that from the concurrence of original, artistic presentation and the handling of the apparatus in the interest of art there emerges an artistic product of a new and specific quality, whose rank derives from the highly qualified contributions from both sources. The two constituent accom-plishments are not interchangeable: the high-standard artistic perform-ance will be impaired by an inferior performance of sound control, and an inferior artistic performance before the microphone cannot be improved by the most ingenious technical accomplishments.

This is not meant in any way to curtail the primacy of the artistic, just as the artist ought not to negate the contribution of sound control to the realization of a work for the medium, a trend prevailing in the copyright sector related to this field. Composers and musicians ought to be aware that the "Tonmeister", particularly when he has undergone high-standard musical training, will understand his job as that of an advocate of their very interests. Many performing artists have long recognized this fact and have gone into partnership with the "Tonmeister", an arrangement that in future should also become effective outside the production process proper, namely when it comes to the representation of subordinate interests.

The musical production process is intervowen with a network of diverse demands centering on the "Tonmeister". Apart from the interpretative and/or creative contribution, which according to the above, he makes to the outcome of the production process – which has to be viewed as an integrated whole – by employing the technical means at his disposal, he has also an artistic responsibility, arising from the fact that in a production – in contrast to a performance in the concert hall – he maintains a permanent critical dialogue with the performers. In this way he can exert an influence on the realization of a work, which is not noticeable from outside. He has his share in an optimalization process before the microphone, which he carries on in the control room by selecting and cross-cutting successful takes.

As studio manager, on the other hand, he is responsible for technical operations and for a labour-saving realization of a production, and it depends on his skill and his personality, whether he is able to strike a balance between the interests of everyone concerned.

In addition to all that, there is a sometimes intangible psychological component to his work, which is least visible in the finished phonogram. In the very often sterile atmosphere of a studio production, the "Tonmeister" supported by his team, is the person to whom the interpreters relate their performance. He is not only appreciated as a constructive critic and partner, he is also expected to keep an open mind and to show understanding for all the problems involved in an artistic performance, while at the same time having the strength and charisma to solve critical situations. The complexity of these elements and the uniform whole of the final outcome create a situation for the "Tonmeister" that is comparable to that of a conductor. Just like the conductor he has to inspire the performances of individuals, assessing their limits, and to coordinate them into a common whole.

On the Copyright Situation of the "Tonmeister"

The question of the "Tonmeister's" position with respect to copyright arose, when phonogram manufacturers and performers, prompted by the reproducibility of the communicated product, started to utilize their own performance and also that claimed by sound control, i.e. by the

"Tonmeister", through one of the collecting societies (Gesellschaft zur Verwertung von Leistungsschutzrechten m.b.H., GVL) founded by the bodies representing their interests (German branch of the International Federation of the Phonographic Industry and Deutsche Orchestervereinigung e.V.).

Regarding the practices prevailing in the field of pop-music production, there arises the additional question to what extent the work of the "Tonmeister" is that of a co-author or arranger. In individual cases this question has so far been solved within the scope of the Gesellschaft für musikalische Aufführungs- und mechanische Vervielfältigungsrechte – GEMA (Society for Musical Performance and Mechanical Reproduction Rights).

Apart from doubts raised at the level of legal philosophy and systematics, the difficulties of recognizing the "Tonmeister's" claims are usually referable to the fact that he works as an employee. Generally speaking there are two employment models:

a) The "Tonmeister" as employee of a radio organization or a big record company: In this case, he assigns his copyrights and neighbouring rights to his employer by way of the employment contract. From the declaration of assignment it is obvious that the individual employers consider it possible that such rights may arise and secure them against any possible claims without recognizing them expressis verbis. In the phonographic industry copyrights and neighbouring rights pass to the phonogram manufacturer who compensates his employees with a lump-sum payment. The same procedure is adopted by broadcasting organizations, when the results of the "Tonmeister's" work are used for broadcasting purposes. If these results or products are passed on to a commercial user, the broadcasting organizations are obliged under an industrial agreement providing for the participation of employees in the profit accruing from the utilization of a product, to distribute a share (now 15%) of the total net profit (gross income minus distribution costs and taxes incurred through the utilization) to a group of beneficiaries, which includes employees who are covered by the industry-wide agreement and are authors or contributors in accordance with § 370 of this agreement. Their number includes "Tonmeister" and "Toningenieure" of broadcasting organizations, which means a de facto recognition as artistic contributors at the level of employment contracts and industrial agreements.

b) The "Tonmeister" in a services enterprise (private studio): From the entrepreneur's point of view, the "Tonmeister" is primarily a technician, who has to guarantee the smooth functioning of the equipment. In this capacity he is (with or without contract) tied to the entrepreneur and there is no saying if the latter will be prepared to receive copyrights and neighbouring rights that his employee may become entitled to, as an assignment or if he will claim them himself in his capacity of phonogram manufacturer. The producer, who makes a production in such a services enterprise, hires the production unit together with the production equipment. In his view this includes the operating staff. The experienced producer will know perfectly well that it is not simply a question of operating the equipment, but that the quality and success of his production will largely depend on the creative potential of the respective "Tonmeister". But this is neither part of the contract concluded between the studio owner and the producer, nor is it regulated by the "Tonmeister's" employment contract (if there is such a contract). In this triangular contractual situation the "Tonmeister" has no possibility whatsoever of establishing any legal claim. The general sense of justice shows a growing tendency towards stipulating a regulation. We know of individual cases in which such regulations were made, providing for special fees, premiums or participation in sales for the "Tonmeister". Though they may well be suited to satisfy individual wishes, they will certainly not solve the fundamental legal question.

As far as the protection of neighbouring rights is concerned, one will have to examine whether the "Tonmeister" is a "performing artist" in accordance with § 73 of the Act on Copyright and Related Protective Rights (Gesetz über Urheberrecht und verwandte Schutzrechte – UrhG) of September 9, 1965, an idea which the GVL is principally not prepared to accept.

According to this Act, a performing artist is a person "who presents or performs a work or makes an artistic contribution to the presentation or performance of a work". It follows that the object has to be a "work". There can be no doubt, that all objects to whose realization the "Tonmeister" contributes, are "works" in the above sense. This applies to works of music as well as to TV or radio plays.

Only in exceptional cases will the "Tonmeister" take part in a "performance" in the sense of a public, personal presentation, e.g. in the performance of electronic music or more often in remote contributions during stage performances, etc. The function typically fulfilled by the "Tonmeister" is much rather a "contribution" in accordance with the alternative offered in the second half of the sentence quoted from § 73 of the Copyright Act of the Federal Republic of Germany. Contributors are all those who make a causal contribution to the work. The "Tonmeister" contributes to the realization of an acoustic work of art with the help of electro-acoustic equipment and is thus a contributor.

The contribution has to be an "artistic" one. If it is limited to the reproduction of an interpreter's performance, it will be merely "techni-cal". Operating the technical equipment (playing tapes, operating ma-chines, guaranteeing the smooth technical functioning of the recording apparatus, etc.) no doubt constitutes a technical contribution. But also a musical instrument, just like a mixing console, is a technical instrument. Although the "Tonmeister" cannot "play" his instrument, it does offer him a certain scope of individual, intellectual and aesthetic action. With his instrument he cannot produce sounds as with a musical instrument, but he can exert a lasting influence on the balance between individual instrument groups thus bringing them into a musically meaningful relation.

The performer before the microphone is in no position to commit the "Tonmeister" in advance to specific modalities of sound control. For this reason and because "Tonmeister" and musician are always acting at the same time, the latter necessarily depends on the "Tonmeister's" discretion in employing the means suitable for their joint production, which takes the form of a technical sound event. This is perfectly in keeping with the fact that, if several repeats are made, the primary creator of sound will select the version he considers best.

The artistic function of the "Tonmeister" is certified by an — unpublished — decision of the Schleswig-Holstein Fiscal Court (III 143 – 144/67) of September 18, 1969, which had to deal with the problem from the viewpoint of tax privileges for free-lance artistic work in accordance with § 34, Para. 4, Income-Tax Law. It is largely based on an expert opinion referring to an example of orchestral music and says essentially the following: What is fundamentally new about modern transmission techniques is the fact that the transmitted music develops an artistic life of its own. The placement of a few microphones will not suffice to communicate the intricately structured musical event in the concert hall by creating an approximately similar sound field in the room where it is listened to. This depends essentially on the aesthetic intention of the "Tonmeister", who tries to follow the specific intentions of the composer and the conductor. The "Tonmeister" has a decisive influence on the colour of the recording, which is defined by aesthetic criteria. The "Tonmeister" is, therefore, expected and required to have considerable musical talent and a training equal to that of a conductor. His work must be valued as an independent artistic performance.

As to the individual scope of action, the expert opinion remarks that the recordings of individual "Tonmeister" have specific, aesthetic valencies which — when compared with the original playing — lend them the significance of independent, individual realizations.

The same conclusion is reached in another — unpublished — decision of June 6, 1968, by the District Court of Berlin-Köpenick (16 AG 50/67), which counts the "Tonmeister" as one of the ensemble, in accordance with § 73, 2 of the Copyright Act of the German Democratic Republic. According to this decision and the underlying expert opinion of the

Ministry of Culture and the Musicological Institute of the Humboldt University, the "Tonmeister's" work is "artistically qualified", if it is not only concerned with the faultless technical realization of a musical performance but also with questions of how to interpret the individual work of art. The function of the "Tonmeister" is characterized as "contributing to the artistic rendering", as being one of the causes that make "the recording in its individual stages and as a whole into a work of art that is filled with life".

In a decision of the Hanseatic Higher Regional Court, Hamburg, of May 20, 1974 (3U 190/75) the work of the "Tonregisseur" in the play "Staatstheater" by Kagel is recognized as artistic and equal to that of a soloist.

The "Tonmeister's" work certainly goes beyond a merely technical contribution to the realization of musical works through electro-acoustic media. Though, originally, sound recordings were understood as purely technical operations, which could be rightfully contrasted with the accomplishment of the "performing artist", the development of the past 20 years has enforced a change in this conception. The function of the "Tonmeister" in the technical-artistic transformation process has assumed a weight that has endowed it with predominantly artistic features going hand in hand with high personal-artistic qualifications. This artistic qualification was the criterium for excluding certain occupations, previously running under similar titles, which have retained their purely technical character, e.g. the assistant sound staff. With the growing importance of the technical media, which have even entered the sphere of public performances, the "Tonmeister" has gained considerable influence on the work itself. It is largely up to him, whether the aesthetic intentions of the composer and the conductor or even of the radio-play author and director are or are not correctly reflected in the end product. This is a responsibility of which the "Tonmeister" cannot be relieved by the conductor. The spatial separation alone will permit only limited and in any case subsequent interference. The conductor's possibilities of influencing the "Tonmeister" are much smaller than those of influencing the musicians in the orchestra, who are both in the positive and the negative sense less responsible for the success than the "Tonmeister"; because his influence goes beyond altering such important parameters as the balance of different instrumental groups and their specific dynamics, penetrating much deeper into the realm of artistic expression than that of an experienced orchestral musician. This does not preclude that the final responsibility for the work rests with the conductor. He may reject the one or the other take, just as he may repeat a certain passage with the musicians. But in the end he will depend on the cooperation of the "Tonmeister", if he wishes to attain a creditable result. On the other hand, it is quite usual for the "Tonmeister" to interrupt a studio recording to point out faults that become manifest in his acoustic picture, and to ask for a repetition.

The score or the performance script, its content and correct interpretation, are the actual working material of the "Tonmeister", compared to which the electronic controls and readings hold the subordinate position of hand tools.

The contribution of the "Tonmeister" to the realization of the work is, therefore, predominantly artistic, thus meeting the requirements of § 73 of the Copyright Act of the Federal Republic of Germany.

Karl Breh

High Fidelity, Stereophony, and the Mutation of Musical Communication*

At the beginning of our century, musical communication was still tied to the unity of time and place: it was neither possible to transmit a musical event simultaneously from one place to another, nor was it possible to have a time lag between the musical event and its reception. Performers and audiences had to get together to make acoustic musical communication possible. The reading of scores or the studying of piano scores at the instrument are excluded from this paper, as they are forms of musical communication reserved to the musician.

What was needed to overcome the unity of time and place were the inventions of Edison and Berliner, i.e. the possibility to record sound events and to reproduce them at any time and in any place. Though these inventions were made in the last quarter of the 19th century, it was only around 1900 – and typically enough stimulated by the worldwide popularity of an artist, namely Caruso – that the development they had initiated became something of an industry. Another 20 years had to pass before it became possible to lift the restriction of place, while retaining the unity of time, i.e. to transmit a musical event from the place of performance to one or many other places without any time lag – which became possible with the invention of radio.

With the invention and general introduction of the shellac record and of radio, around the mid-twenties, musical communication was freed from the coercive unity of place and time. Musical events could be recorded, duplicated and reproduced in any place and at any time; in addition they could be transmitted on electro-magnetic waves and simultaneously received in all places within the transmitter's range. This was the point, when in principle all the possibilities now existing in the audio field were

---

* The collection of data presented in this paper was completed in 1979.

available. The differences to the present state of affairs, though merely of a qualitative and quantitative order, are nevertheless profound.

Musical Communication

What is musical communication? Is it effected by communicating a melody, a harmonic or rhythmic structure, agogics or tempo? Communication of this type may well suffice to offer the more or less expert listener insight into fundamental interpretative idiosyncrasies, e.g. of an Artur Nikisch conducting the Berlin Philharmonic in 1913, and we would wish to have similar, scant documents of Gustav Mahler's conducting or Paganini's violin playing. But from those early acoustic documents we certainly get no real impression of what the Berlin Philharmonic sounded like in 1913. Radio was subject to similar quality restrictions before the introduction of frequency modulation in the 50s. It was FM-radio that finally did away with the nuisance of atmospherics and already then had a bandwidth of 40 to 15.000 Hz, which has been considered sufficient for radio to this very day.

Qualitative improvement of the record started earlier and in smaller steps, which can be indicated by the catchwords: replacement of acoustic recording by electro-acoustic recording via microphones (1925); invention of the electron tube and consequent possibility of amplification (1904/25); recording on magnetic tape with the possibility of montage, which permitted more economical production (1946); introduction of the LP (1951) and introduction of stereophony (1958). During the 50s the overall concept of "high fidelity" came to embrace, first in the USA and Great Britain and later on also in Japan and in the industrialized countries of the European continent, all the gradually achieved technical improvements in sound recording, in the production of phonograms, in their duplication and in the development and manufacture of reproducing equipment, the sum total of which ushered in the mutation of musical communication.

Development of the Hi-Fi Market

In the 50s the development of the hi-fi market in the Federal Republic of Germany was sluggish; in the 60s it gathered momentum to become downright impetuous in the second half of the 70s. Let me give a few figures in evidence. The statistics of the Association of Entertainment Electronics in the Central Union of the Electrotechnical Industry (Fachverband Unterhaltungselektronik im Zentralverband der Elektrotechnischen Industrie), which, however, covers only domestic production, disregarding imports which play such an important role, particularly in the hi-fi sector, shows that in 1966 about 57,000 receivers had been produced to the DIN 45 500 standard (German hi-fi standard). In 1970 the figure had risen to over 300,000, in 1972 to about 380,000. In 1978 the number dropped to 250,000, following the reverse trend back to separate components. The corresponding figures for amplifiers, evidencing the same trend, are: 30,000 for 1966, 58,000 for 1970, 93,000 for 1972, and about 154,000 for 1978. The production figures for tuners run parallel: around 17,000 in 1966, around 133,000 in 1978; the figures for amplifiers and tuners also include equipment not meeting the DIN 45 500 standard, but again exclude imports, which are so very important for this type of equipment. This year, total sales of hi-fi equipment in the Federal Republic and West Berlin may, according to reliable estimates, well exceed 3,000 million DM, which would mean a 16% increase as compared with the past year. Sales increases in the same order of magnitude are again expected next year, since the market saturation in the Federal Republic and West Berlin is hardly above 35%. Market saturations are related to the number of households, which means that the number of people satisfying their music demand through the medium of high fidelity, is much higher than the number of concert-goers, including pop concerts and open-air festivals.

Interesting inferences can also be drawn from the development of journals and magazines on high fidelity. Four year ago, "fono forum" and "HiFi-Stereophonie", with a total circulation of 50,000, were the only two journals in the Federal Republic devoted to high fidelity, record reviews and related subjects; today, "Stereo", "Audio", "HiFi-Exklusiv",[1] "Klangbild",[1] and "stereoplay" have raised the number to seven, with a total circulation of well over 200,000. It is characteristic that the newly founded publications of varying standard are mainly concerned with technical questions, and if music or record reviews are offered at all, they are mostly related to the popular species that are more likely to find the interest of broader population strata. One counterweight to these stereotypes can be seen in the fact that practically all supra-regional dailies and weeklies, but also smaller papers of regional importance as well as the big magazines, regularly carry contributions on high fidelity as well as record reviews, that usually are of a higher standard. No doubt, this has mobilized ever broader population strata for high fidelity. The interest of young people, who grow up with hi-fi technology, is further enhanced by the continued pop-music boom, triggered by the Beatles.

Ten years ago, only a negligible percentage of the population knew what is hidden behind the terms "high fidelity" and "stereophony", being quite incapable of telling the difference between the two; a representative inquiry conducted among the visitors to a regional weekend exhibition

---

[1] These two magazines ceased to exist in 1981.

(May 1979), which the German High Fidelity Institute has arranged three to four times a year, for the past seven years, showed that 82.5% of those questioned did know the difference between high fidelity and stereophony. A similarly high rate of information was indicated by a pertinent study of the Gesellschaft für Konsum- und Marktforschung (Society for Consumption and Market Research).

It is evident that the outlined development has had and will have considerable repercussions on the phonographic industry. The following figures are designed to substantiate this statement and to show up interesting trends. Total sales of the companies comprised by the Bundesverband der Phonographischen Wirtschaft (Federal Association of the Phonographic Industry) amounted to 709 million DM in 1970, and to 2,110 million DM in 1978. If the 1970 index is assumed to equal 100, the corresponding figure for 1978 was 255.8. During the same period the index for singles rose from 100 to 127.7, that for LPs from 100 to 267.2 and that for musicassettes from 100 to 2,247.3 (!), for LPs and MCs together from 100 to 361.3. 112.5 million LPs, 47.2 million musicassettes and 46.5 million singles were sold in 1978, which means that in numbers the musicassette has overtaken the single, while the percentage of MCs sold related to that of LPs sold is 41.95%. If one adds up the number of LPs and MCs sold in 1978 and relates the figure to the total, the LPs' share in sales is 70.4%, that of the MCs 29.4%. A clear trend is also evidenced by the percentile shares of serious and light music. In 1970, serious music – at that time still without musicassettes – had an 18.5% share in sales, with 7.8 million LPs being sold. In 1978 the share of serious music (LPs plus MCs) had dropped to 10.8%, though 17.2 million units or by 220% more serious music phonograms were sold than in 1970. Unfortunately, the statistics offer no figures indicating the share of musicassettes in serious music. But we do know that in 1977 30% of 100 newly released LPs, produced either in Germany or abroad, belonged to the serious music repertoire.

Cassette Recorders and Radio Programmes

Two important factors must be considered, when trying to assess the impact of music produced and sold by phonogram manufacturers: The growing use of high-quality cassette recorders has, particularly in the pop sector, led to a lively exchange of commercially produced phonograms among consumers, for the purpose of re-recording them on blank cassettes. Also radio programmes with pop and serious music can be and are recorded on blank cassettes, practically without loss of quality. The acoustic quality of such recordings is in general better than that of recorded musicassettes marketed by the industry, because they do not suffer from the shortcomings of large-batch copying, though it must be admitted that considerable progress has been made in this field during the past two years. Of the approximately 80 million blank cassettes sold in the Federal Republic of Germany and in West Berlin in 1978 — which is almost double the number of recorded cassettes sold during the same period — a very high percentage may be assumed to have been used for recording commercially produced music. This explains the demand of GEMA (Gesellschaft für musikalische Aufführungs- und mechanische Vervielfältigungsrechte — Society for Musical Performance and Mechanical Reproduction Rights) for a copyright fee to be paid for each blank cassette sold, though one must add that such a fee is already being collected on each tape or cassette recorder that is sold. The second point to be considered is the fact that a large share of the music programmes offered by the German broadcasting stations draw on this source. Even Südwestfunk Baden-Baden, with a symphony orchestra of its own and with its own music productions in almost all fields of serious music except opera, reports a 55 to 60% share of records in serious music programmes. In the pop sector the percentage of records is probably much higher. In the serious music sector, the loss of phonogram manufacturers due to re-recordings is certainly over-compensated by music lovers buying new records which they get to know through radio programmes that frequently offer excerpts only. In the much shorter-lived pop sector the situation will probably be reversed, but it is almost impossible to get hold of reliable figures.

The Second Way of Musical Communication

The mentioned figures may have shown up the quantitative difference between the situation of technically communicated music in the pre-hi-fi era and today. Music of all genres and from all historical epochs has become available without restrictions of time and place, to an extent nobody would have dreamed of, thirty years ago. This ubiquity of music, its dissemination in first-rate interpretations to the depths of the backwoods and the remotest mountain village, cannot be achieved by way of direct musical communication. The live concert is tied to urban infrastructures or, in their absence, at least to historically grown or artificially established cultural centres. Direct musical communication will always be a local, "pin-point" event, which can only be realized within an organized community. The quality of what is offered has, at least since the abolition of feudal structures, been proportional to the potential audiences that can be mobilized. For towns with populations of less than 200,000, the range of the repertoire and its artistic presentation will, apart from occasional exceptions, drop to a provincial standard in the worst sense of the term. Where, outside Vienna or London, is anybody offered a chance of acquainting himself with all the symphonies by Gustav Mahler within a period of ten years; and where, outside a few big cities, and although it would actually be much easier to arrange, will one find performance cycles offering all Beethoven's string quartets or pianoforte sonatas? He who depends on direct musical communication or – which today seems the only reason – insists on it, has no possibility of getting really well acquainted with music. This refers to the repertoire and to the knowledge of one single work, alike. There is no denying that the live concert may leave lasting or even unforgettable impressions, which are often created merely by the presence of the artist or artists and by the immediate experience of being part of an enthusiastic audience. But for the intimate knowledge of a work it will be necessary to listen to it more often than once and for an understanding of its scope and substance one will have to compare different interpretations. This is the very point, where the fascinating medium of hi-fi stereophony comes in, that second way of music listening and musical communication.

A striking mutation has taken place in musical communication. The live concert has been assigned a complementary role, fulfilling its traditional social function and satisfying the need of "mutated" connoisseurs, who have become intimately familiar with artists through their technically communicated interpretations, to hear and see them also in concert, or as it were, in the flesh. This function may, by the way, be taken over with growing success and with a growing cultural demand by the audio-visual media.

Before going on to describe the artistic-cultural categories of the new medium and their transforming effect on musical communication, we have to define the difference in technical quality between what existed thirty years ago and what is offered today. Thirty years ago, technically communicated music provided nothing but a rough pattern, full of defects and disturbances, of the information content making up a work. In other words, the fractional communication of content was in addition partly obscured, changed and distorted by interferences. In those days, technically communicated music had little more than sentimental value: Those who were already familiar with a work, added from their memories what was missing, obscured or distorted in the reproduction. Those unacquainted with it, got at least a rough pattern of primary information.

Today, the situation is fundamentally different: hi-fi reproduction, be it from radio, record or tape, supplies the total frequency range relevant to the music. With record and tape it is even larger than required. The whole frequency spectrum covered by the music is transmitted and – what is equally important – there is not only nothing taken away, i.e. there are no information gaps, but there is nothing added either, i.e. no timbre-changing overtones, no atmospherics, no humming noise, no distortion.

The only restrictions relate to dynamics, i.e. the ratio between the loudest and the lowest passages. This ratio, expressed in decibel, can in case of a big symphony orchestra in a concert hall reach the extreme value of 80 dB, or in linear terms 1 : 10,000. The loudest passage will then reach a level of 120 dB which is the pain threshold of human hearing. The lowest passage would have 40 dB. Whispering or rustling leaves have a level of 30 dB, so that even in very quiet surroundings the ambient noise will exceed 40 dB. Thus, the dynamics of a big orchestra must inevitably be reduced to a reasonable level, when transmitting to a smaller room. With radio a dynamic range of 40 dB is considered the upper limit, with particularly sophisticated records it is 45 to 50 dB. As a rule, such a compression of dynamics does not entail an adulteration of the musical message, because the skilful handling of the control desk during the recording process will preserve the contrasting effect of fortissimo and pianissimo also in the reproduction in another room. If a dynamic range of 80 dB were to be transmitted without compression to the room where the music is listened to, the listener would have to reduce the volume during loud passages and increase it again during low ones, as pianissimo passages would otherwise be drowned by the ambient noise. For these psychoacoustic reasons the dynamics will also have to be compressed, if the technically communicable dynamic range should in the near future exceed even the extreme value of 80 dB. Pop music is not affected by this problem, as it usually has a much smaller dynamic range.

Today, high fidelity — at least under optimum, certainly attainable conditions — means unadulterated reproduction in any acoustic room, so that deviations from the original can, at best, be spotted by direct comparison or by means of measurement. The possibility of manipulation during the recording process, which may be motivated by the aesthetic sound conception of either the recording team or the performing artist, has nothing to do with the technical quality of the medium, i.e. with the quality of the transmission.

Space and Music

High fidelity, that is to say high quality of transmission, is a necessary but in itself insufficient precondition for assigning to technically communicated music the rank of a universal, independent medium. Kurt Blaukopf has coined the apt metaphor of space as the garment of music. In this context space has a dual meaning. On the one hand it refers to the room in which the music is played: concert hall, church, opera house and, in the case of transmissions, the room where it is listened to. On the other hand, every orchestra or ensemble has a certain structure in space. For instance the seating order of a symphony orchestra, which would be a static arrangement, or the dynamic structure of choirs, ensembles or individual scenes in opera performances. Both types of spatiality determine to a greater or lesser extent the acoustic impression received by the listener. Both are as far as possible to be projected into the room where the transmission is listened to. This is in part achieved by stereophony, by imitating two-eared listening when recording and by doubling the transmission channels. The spatial structure of the orchestra or ensemble can be very exactly reproduced in its width and more or less precisely in its depth. This lends greater transparency to the sound event. In addition, directional hearing makes it possible to acoustically reproduce movement in opera performances. The interaction between the orchestra and the surfaces enclosing the room in which it is recorded, that is to say the modifications of the auditive impression effected by the acoustics of the recording room, can be much better transmitted by a stereophonic than a monaural reproduction. What remains inevitable is an interaction between the acoustics of the recording room as part of the recording and the acoustics of the room where it is listened to. The normal sound volumes of large orchestras or ensembles will be annoying in too small rooms. An almost ideal possibility of transmitting the acoustics of the recording room to the individual listening room concomitant with a marked reduction in the influence of the listening room's special acoustics, is offered by quadraphony, which unfortunately – for reasons whose analysis would go beyond the scope of this paper – was unable to make a breakthrough at the first attempt, in the period between 1972 and 1975. Correct quadraphonic reproduction will transform a room of only 20 to 30 sqm into a church aisle, an opera house or a chamber music hall, by supplying the acoustics of the recording room as part of the recording. This, in itself, is an invaluable advantage. But in addition, quadraphony opens up new dimensions of artistic creation and forms of expression, that are difficult or impossible to realize in live concerts. In this light it appears unlikely that quadraphony will not make a breakthrough as soon as it has achieved technical perfection in connection with new developments that may be subsumed under the term "digitalization", and as soon as it will no longer be suffering from a confusion of systems.

Autonomy of the Medium

High fidelity and two or four-channel stereophony are the necessary and adequate prerequisites for an autonomous medium for the technical communication of music. The gradual improvement of these prerequisites over the past 25 years and their incorporation into equipment at an increasingly favourable price/quality ratio, enabled this autonomous medium of musical communication to attain the importance indicated by the above-mentioned figures. This development has led to a mutation in musical communication, opening up a second way of experiencing music, beside music-making in the home and concert-going. To many, this medium has become the primary means and to some – deplorably or not? – the only means of encountering and getting to the depth of music. The success of this technical line of musical communication would be almost unimaginable, were it not to fulfil two media-specific criteria: impartiality and universality. Hi-fi stereophony is an impartial medium, because it is open to all species and types of music, from serious music via jazz and pop, operetta and musical comedy to the ephemeral hit. It is at the disposal of good and bad music alike. There is no "valuation filter" attached to the medium, and it is universally applicable. But whenever it is used with cultural intent, it is subject to relevant criticism. As the medium is also autonomous, the criticism relevant to it must be medium-specific. The meaning behind this statement will be more clearly revealed by some examples of the medium's autonomy.

By employing suitable recording techniques the technically communicated performance of musical works may be rendered superior to that in the concert hall. The reason lies in the fact that the two ears of the listener in the concert hall can be replaced by as many microphones as are deemed necessary for the optimum recording of a musical work. In such recordings, acoustic defects of the recording room are eliminated by technical means and an ideal balance can be established between the individual instrument groups. Just think of certain operas, where there is always a risk of the singers being drowned by the orchestra, if the conductor strictly observes the dynamics indications. When a performance is recorded in stereo, vocal soloists and the choir have their own microphones, which makes it possible – while observing the composer's intentions – to make singers, orchestra and chorus equally audible. Or another example: for economic reasons, string quartets very often have to play in far too large halls. The listeners in the back rows will not be able to fully enjoy the musical nuances, which often are the main attraction of string quartets, or may, indeed, run the risk of not hearing the pianissimo passages at all. Hi-fi stereophony is capable of transmitting a string quartet as naturally and transparently, as if the artists were playing in the listener's home, the only difference being that the room acoustics are even improved by the recording. Though I could name an infinite number of similar examples, I shall simply state one fact: The well-understood aim of hi-fi stereo-reproduction is not to picture a concert hall with its positive and negative characteristics, but to bring every musical work into being in its optimum and thus adequate acoustic form. The crucial point is to keep the use of technical means subject to artistic control, so that the outcome may not be in direct contradiction to the composer's intentions. This is also the goal and the criterium on which expert, medium-oriented criticism will be based.

Further evidence of the medium's autonomy is furnished by the selection of artists engaged for a recording and by the possibility of eliminating any flaws caused by indisposition, which would be neither possible nor necessary in the concert hall, where we experience a unique event. A record, on the other hand, can be played whenever desired, it has the character of a document rather than of a spontaneous event. Even the slightest flaw, if it keeps recurring in the same place, will in the long run be annoying. For this reason the record has, as far as possible, also to strive for artistic perfection. Fortunately, any imperfection can be corrected by cutting the magnetic tape and fitting in a flawless repeat of the passage in question. Thus it will rarely happen that a work was played the way the recording will later on have us believe. Though the artists will have played or sung all the sounds that are heard, they will not have done so in an uninterrupted performance and hardly in the correct order. One might regard this as something of a counterfeit; but any such allegation must be dropped, the moment one accepts the fact that the record in conjunction with hi-fi stereophony is an autonomous medium governed by laws of artistic production which differ profoundly from those applying to a live performance in the concert hall. The record is no document of the artist's infallibility under live conditions, but much rather proof of his capability to reach artistic perfection – furnished by using the production conditions and possibilities in the studio. This is another criterium for expert record criticism.

The user of the medium may not be fully aware of these interconnections. This was the reason why the German High Fidelity Institute arranged concert production workshops within the framework of the "Hi-Fi '78 – International Exhibition and Festival, Düsseldorf". With the assistance of the EMI production team, who had set up a complete control cubicle in an adjoining room which was open to the public, and with the help of powerful hi-fi equipment and of colour TV-monitors that established a visual connection between concert hall and control room, the differences between recorded and live performances were demonstrated to the public in six concerts. The performances were all divided up into a production part and a live part. The artists, questioned by a moderator, talked about the different working conditions and voiced their opinions from the artistic point of view. Even the editing technique was visually and acoustically demonstrated to the audience. One movement from each work, which later on also received a complete live performance, was produced under the same conditions as a disc recording. Direct comparison of the live performance and the recording played to the concert hall via the hi-fi equipment, permitted also a qualitative comparison. The recordings produced in these workshops have been released on discs. The experiment met with such a lively response from everyone involved that similar concert production workshops are planned to be arranged again within the framework of "Hi-Fi '80".

The autonomy of the medium becomes also manifest in opera productions. For a disc recording one can engage – if no obstacles are raised by tiresome exclusive contracts, which fortunately are on the decrease – the vocal soloists best suited for each part, while even the most famous opera houses in the world – not to mention provincial theatres – are subject to budgetary and repertoire restrictions and have to work with more or less permanent ensembles. Furthermore, there are entire musical areas, from early music played on original instruments to new music which is either impossible or too expensive to perform in concert halls or is never played for repertoire reasons, that owe their revitalization or dissemination to radio and record. The repertoire offered on discs and to a certain extent on radio to anyone interested, no matter whether he lives in a big town or in a remote rural village, is extremely variegated. With very few exceptions it comprises the music of the world from its beginnings to its newest forms, mostly in several renderings by the best artists available. Hi-fi stereophony as an autonomous and neutral medium has ensured a dissemination of music that would have been called utopian only a few decades ago. In this way it has done and is doing much more to extend the social range of music and to enhance its humanizing impact than all the public temples dedicated to it, like concert halls and opera houses, put together.

Changing Listening Behaviour

The above may have served to show that the medium changes the musical message in a specific manner, which is usually in the interest of the work. In any case, there is absolute concentration on the auditive, because compared with communication in the concert hall, the visual component which often conveys interpretative intentions without musical counter-part, is totally lacking. This fact is reflected in a changed listening behaviour. The absence of the visual component, on the one hand, acoustic perfection and transparency of the sound event, on the other hand, enhance and virtually induce the individual listener's readiness to concentrate. The listening situation of the individual in front of his hi-fi set differs profoundly from that of the same individual sharing the com-munity of an audience in a live performance. His attention is more strongly concentrated on the purely musical component.

The medium transcends the borders of live music both in terms of repertoire and in acoustic terms. With traditional, serious music the possibilities are relatively modest, usually — if we leave aside the opera that has already been dealt with — affecting instrumental balance. In disc recordings of concertos, particularly of violin concertos, the solo instrument is, as a rule, more strongly accentuated than is possible in the concert hall. As a result, "mutated" music lovers will occasionally be disappointed by the markedly reduced sonority, when they hear their favourite violinist playing a work in the concert hall, which they know from a record.

In the case of new music, and particularly of electronic compositions, the medium is the natural choice for an acoustic emancipation from the possibilities of live performance. But curiously enough, many elements of new music are designed in a way that absolutely necessitates the visual component, lest there should occur a loss of substance. Whether this is an indicator of scant musical substance in some of these compositions, is a moot point.

Pop music is most consistent in utilizing the emancipatory potential of the medium. There are innumerable pieces which will never sound in a live performance as they sound when played from a record on a hi-fi equipment. Pop music creatively employs the inexhaustible technical resources of the medium to generate new sounds and timbres, employing primarily electronics and synthesizers. What in a live pop concert all too often degenerates into distorted and deafening noise, may reveal itself as imaginative music, rich in nuances, when played from a record on a hi-fi equipment.

Prognosis

What will the future have in store? Inspite of the profound technological changes that are under way and will probably be concluded before the year 2000, the medium will rather change in terms of quantity than quality. The technical quality achieved with the still generally used analogue recording and transmission techniques has, in its best and of course most expensive and far from average forms, for years asymptotically approached absolute perfection. The replacement of the analogue by the digital technique will, therefore, only bring minor improvements, hardly discernible by the ear. The unweighted signal-to-noise ratios will certainly rise to over 80 dB, and records that are scanned inertia and contact-free by a laser beam, will produce neither crackling nor clicking noises, nor any other surface-generated disturbance and will not suffer from wear. But their acoustics can't possibly be much further improved. The record of the future will admittedly be much smaller in size, with a diameter of only 120 mm, and although only one side will be used, it will have a playing time of one hour. All this, on the condition that the Philips compact record, which has already been internationally presented, will be adopted as universal standard, which is still far from guaranteed. In Japan, for instance, one tends to adopt a size for the digital audio-record that is compatible with the respective video system. Though, personally, I would consider this a regrettable misdevelopment, it cannot be precluded. In any case, even if in the development laboratories the sobering effect of quadraphony's initial failure prohibits any thought of reintroducing discrete four-channel stereophony in the course of digitalization – which will then be possible without compromises – I have no doubt that quadraphony will have a comeback sooner or later. As indicated, such a revival would also have qualitative consequences for the medium, in the sense of opening up a new spatial dimension and of a further emancipation from live music. Equipment manufacturers will certainly try to concentrate the audio-visual medium in one communication centre, i.e. to integrate the TV-set or better the screen and the video recorder into the audio equipment, or vice versa, depending on the point of departure. Nobody can foretell to what extent the public will take up what is offered, or whether the majority will adopt a critical attitude, demanding from television "the things that are television's", but not wishing for moving pictures when consciously listening to music, either because they want to leave the visual element to their imagination or because they prefer to concentrate on the auditive. Presumably it will be as ever and everywhere: "Who bringeth much will something bring to everyone."

ANNEX I

List of Experts Cooperating in the Project

Anderson, Robert D., Canada, Statistics Canada, Ottawa.

Arming, Wolfgang, Austria, Polygram Austria, Vienna.

Beaud, Paul, France/Switzerland, Institut de Sociologie des Communications de Masse, Université de Lausanne.

Bontinck, Irmgard, Austria, Assistant Director of Research, MEDIACULT.

Brans, Bernard M., Netherlands, Katholieke radio omroep [KRO], Hilversum.

Breh, Karl, FRG, Deutsches High-Fidelity-Institut, Frankfurt.

Corposanto, Cleto, Italy, Facoltà di Sociologia, Libera Università degli Studi di Trento.

Davies, Gillian, Great Britain, International Federation of Producers of Phonograms and Videograms [IFPI], London.

Del Grosso Destreri, Luigi, Italy, Centro per l'educazione musicale e per la sociologia della musica, Trento.

Dienes, Gedeon P., Hungary, Népmüvelési Intézet [Institute for Culture], Budapest.

Etzkorn, K. Peter, U.S.A., Graduate School and Office of Research, University of Missouri, St. Louis.

Ferland, Yvon, Canada, Statistics Canada, Ottawa.

Golovinsky, Grigory, USSR, Institute for Research in the Arts, Moscow.

Ghosh, Avik, India, Centre for the Development of Instructional Technology [CENDIT], New Delhi.

Hennion, Antoine, France, Centre de Sociologie de l'Innovation, Ecole Nationale Supérieure des Mines, Paris.

Lemieux, Gilbert, Canada, Emissions enregistrées, Radio Canada International, Montréal.

Malm, Krister, Sweden, Rikskonserter [Institute for National Concerts], Stockholm.

Mark, Desmond, Austria, Institut für Musiksoziologie, Hochschule für Musik und darstellende Kunst, Vienna.

Ostleitner, Elena, Austria, Institut für Musiksoziologie, Hochschule für Musik und darstellende Kunst, Vienna.

Sági, Mária, Hungary, Népmüvelési Intézet [Institute for Culture], Budapest.

Schlemm, Wilhelm, West-Berlin, Verband Deutscher Tonmeister e.V., West-Berlin.

Schüller, Dietrich, Austria, Phonogrammarchiv der Österreichischen Akademie der Wissenschaften, Vienna.

Signitzer, Benno, Austria, Institut für Publizistik und Kommunikationstheorie, Universität Salzburg.

Steinmetz, Helmut, Austria, Austro-Mechana GmbH., Vienna.

Tomisawa, Kazuma, Japan/Switzerland, International Cultural Exchange Agency, Meyrin-Genève.

Wallis, Roger, Great Britain/Sweden, Department of Musicology, University of Gothenburg.

Wallnöfer, Pierre, Austria, Institut für Publizistik und Kommunikationstheorie, Universität Salzburg.

Weeda, Robert, Netherlands, Music Department, Nederlandse Christelijke Radio Vereiniging [NCRV], Hilversum.

ANNEX II

Contributions Made to the Project Not Contained in this Publication

Beaud, Paul, Industry of the Imaginary. The Present State of Research on Phonograms.

Bontinck, Irmgard, Changes in Cultural Communication [A survey of MEDIACULT research 1969 – 1979].

Brans, Bernard M., Cultural Aims of Sound Radio ["Identifaction" of stations and role of phonograms].

Davies, Gillian, Compulsory Deposit of Sound Recordings.

Dienes, Gedeon P., Videography and Cultural Communication in Hungary.

Schüller, Dietrich, The Accessibility of Non-Commercial Recordings and the Tasks of Sound Archives.

Weeda, Robert, Phonograms in the Programmes of the Dutch Classical Music Channel Hilversum 4.

Computergesteuerter Fotosatz und Umbruch: Dipl.-Ing. Schwarz' Erben KG, A-3910 Zwettl NÖ. — Reproduktion und Offsetdruck: Novographic, Ing. Wolfgang Schmid, A-1230 Wien.

MEDIACULT

International Institute for Audio-visual
Communication and Cultural Development

Institut international pour les communications
audio-visuelles et le développement culturel

Internationales Institut für audio-visuelle
Kommunikation und kulturelle Entwicklung

A-1030 Wien, Metternichgasse 12

Tel. (0222) 72 53 44, 75 12 86   Cables Mediacult Wien

*The Institute was founded in 1969 and is enjoying consultative status
with UNESCO. In the research projects of this international Institute
the following subjects are treated on an interdisciplinary basis.*

New Patterns of Musical Behaviour in Industrial Societies

*The Influence of TV Programs Devoted to Contemporary Plastic Art
upon the Development of Art Galleries*

Cultural Democracy on the Community Level

*The Mutation of Cultural Communication under the Impact of the
Electronic Media*

*Mass Media and the Economic Dilemma of the Performing Arts
Institutions*

President
Robert Wangermée, Brussels

Director
Kurt Blaukopf, Vienna